CW01329462

PRAISE FOR *FINDING FREEDOM IN CHRIST*

"From years of counseling men and women, Dr. Breuninger has a keen sense of what binds people and how the bondage and their woundedness prohibit them from living fully human lives. . . . He provides a model for the reader that leads us to a place of freedom and wholeness. . . . Dr. Breuninger leads us to an encounter with Jesus so we may experience the freedom He has won for us."

FR. DAVE PIVONKA, TOR
President, Franciscan University of Steubenville

"Dr. Matthew Breuninger is a true co-worker of healing in the Lord's vineyard. In *Finding Freedom in Christ*, he beautifully integrates sound psychological science, the wisdom of the Twelve Steps, and the riches of our Catholic faith to chart a sure path for healing. As a result, *Finding Freedom in Christ* will challenge, enlighten, and console readers who hunger for God's healing touch in their lives. I encourage all those hesitating to open this book with the words of Pope St. John Paul II: 'Do not be afraid. Open wide the doors to Christ!'"

ANDREW J. SODERGREN, PSY.D.
Director of Psychological Services, Ruah Woods Institute

"In a world filled with so much woundedness and pain, Dr. Breuninger offers us hope—the hope of Christ! The steps contained in *Finding Freedom in Christ* are practical and powerful, sure to help you shed the shackles of your wounds and bring you into the freedom that God desires for you."

MATT FRADD
Host of the Pints with Aquinas *Podcast*

"Dr. Matthew Breuninger beautifully explores how the wounds we carry, heavy and hurting, can be healed by recognizing and fully embracing God's abundant and perfect love. Without over-spiritualizing the ways to find healing (and making note of the need for mental health professionals), Dr. Breuninger examines how, step by step, we can seek perfect healing not simply by trying hard and grinning and bearing it, but instead by going through a clear process of naming, claiming, and moving beyond the hurts we carry and seeing God for who He is, and thus coming to see ourselves more fully. As someone who deals with anxiety, and regularly goes to therapy, Dr. Breuninger's book provided additional excellent insight into how I can find healing from past hurts and seek comfort in the loving arms of the Lord, who loves me in my woundedness and seeks to bring me beyond it. I loved this book, and think it is a great resource for Catholics longing to find healing."

KATIE PREJEAN MCGRADY
Host of The Katie McGrady Show *on Sirius XM*

FINDING FREEDOM *in* CHRIST

FINDING FREEDOM *in* CHRIST

Healing Life's Hurts

DR. MATTHEW BREUNINGER

EMMAUS ROAD
PUBLISHING

Steubenville, Ohio
www.emmausroad.org

EMMAUS ROAD

Emmaus Road Publishing
1468 Parkview Circle
Steubenville, Ohio 43952

© 2022 Matthew Breuninger
All rights reserved. Published 2022
Printed in the United States of America
Second Printing 2023

Library of Congress Control Number 2022936857
ISBN: 978-1-64585-224-7 Hardcover | 978-1-64585-225-4 Paperback | 978-1-64585-226-1 Ebook

Unless otherwise noted, Scripture quotations are taken from The Revised Standard Version Second Catholic Edition (Ignatius Edition) Copyright © 2006 by the Division of Christian Education of the National Council of the Churches of Christ in the United States of America. Used by permission. All rights reserved.

Excerpts from the Catechism of the Catholic Church, second edition, copyright ©2000, Libreria Editrice Vaticana—United States Conference of Catholic Bishops, Washington, DC. Noted as "CCC" in the text.

Cover design by Emily Morelli
Layout by Cori McCulloch
Cover image: *The Incredulity of Saint Thomas* by Caravaggio, 1603.

*To my love, Britt, and our beautiful children—
Asher, Amelia, Oliver, Benedict, Lucia,
and Charlie. You are gifts that I do not deserve.
There's no other tribe I'd rather be a part of.*

CONTENTS

Acknowledgments	xi
Foreword	xiii
Introduction	xvii
I. Everyone Suffers	1
II. Lose to Win	13
III. A God Who Wants to Heal	25
IV. A Bit about Wounds	43
V. Self-Preservation: Achieving Security by Avoiding Pain	55
VI. Types of Healing & Healing the Conscience	65
VII. Steps One and Two	77
VIII. Steps Three and Four	85
IX. Steps Five and Six	97
X. Restored in Christ—Healing in the Sacraments	107
XI. One Day at a Time	117
Appendix A: Some Common Questions	127
Appendix B: Prayers	141
Appendix C: Worksheet Template	149
Appendix D: Ten Common Thought Errors	151

ACKNOWLEDGMENTS

I'D BE REMISS IF I didn't start by thanking my friend Bill W. for blazing the trail and laying out a path of healing before me. A special thanks to Dad, Mom, and Drew for your love and support. Mom, you are one of the strongest women I know. Your humility, resolve in the face of difficulty, and unflinching willingness to grow constantly are an inspiration to me. To my Nana—your home is like a bed and breakfast for the hurting and broken to bind their wounds and get back on their feet. Thanks for letting me make a pit stop. A big thanks to the Murphys for your constant friendship and encouragement—it has been a *sine qua non*. Shout out to my buddy Kris for reading an early draft of the manuscript and providing me with helpful feedback and sincere encouragement. Finally, thanks to Melissa and all of the staff at Emmaus Road Publishing for helping to bring this work to fruition. If this books helps anyone, it is only because of all those who have helped me. Thank you.

FOREWORD

THE FIRST WORDS out of the mouth of God were: "You are free" (Gen 2:16). God, who is fully free, created the human person out of freedom, so we may share in the freedom that God possesses. All was well in the beginning. Scripture reminds us that in the afternoon, Adam and Eve, who were naked, would take long strolls in the Garden with God as their companion. All was good, and all was right.

But something went terribly wrong. We ate the fruit of that one tree. While we were free to eat of this fruit, we were also asked not to do so. We thought we knew better and partook of the fruit of a single tree, and instantly, we were riddled with shame and regret. We covered ourselves, and we hid from God. "Where are you?" (Gen. 3:9), God would say as he looked for us. Imagine that, God looking for us as we hid from him. Were I God, a scary proposition to be sure, I don't think I would go looking. You want to hide from me? Fine. I'm not going to play your games, not going to humble myself and go looking for you.

Our God is different. He is all about looking for us, looking for the one lost sheep. And what might he want us to know once he finds us? That we are free. God has always wanted his people to know we are free. In the first chapter of Luke, before Jesus has been born, we hear the prophet Zechariah proclaim, "Blessed be the Lord, the God of Israel, he has come to set his people free." Before Jesus has even come to earth, we are getting clarity as to one of the purposes of Jesus' coming. In

John's Gospel we hear, "if the son makes you free, you are free indeed" (John 8:36). And then in Galatians, it boldly states, "For freedom Christ has set us free . . . do not submit again to a yoke of slavery" (Gal. 5:1). We are meant to be free.

As Americans, we think a lot about freedom, and rightly so. It's a part of our DNA. One only needs to spend a few minutes looking at many of our most beloved monuments in Washington, DC, to see the primacy of freedom. I think of the large black wall at the World War II Memorial with 4,048 gold stars, each one representing 100 Americans who died in the war. In front of the wall, in large bold letters, it states, *"Here We Mark the Price of Freedom."*

As moving as this is, it is important to make a distinction. Our ultimate freedom, the freedom we have as human persons, does not come from a government. This is important because it identifies and makes clear the source of our freedom. Freedom is not from a government, a president, or courts. It isn't something we attain by wishing or desiring. Rather, freedom is a gift from God. We are free because this is how God has created us and the salvific work of Christ restored our freedom. We are free because Christ has set us free, not because a government declares us so.

However, too many people miss this point and don't live fully free lives.

There was a famous line from a movie many years ago that went something like "they are dead, and they don't even know it," speaking of people walking around in our midst. My concern is that there are many people who are bound or trapped and don't even know it. So many Christians have become accustomed to their bondage that it has become familiar, and they don't even know there is a different way to live. They "get by" and say things like, "It's not that bad," but they don't know God has so much more for them. This is profoundly sad. God wants us to live as free sons and daughters,

Foreword

but this requires that each of us discover what holds us captive. The list is long—fear, anger, the past, the future, relationships, and sin all hold us captive. But God wants to bring freedom, healing, and wholeness to our brokenness. God wants his people free.

And this is why Dr. Matthew Breuninger's book is such a blessing. Dr. Breuninger believes with all his heart that God wants to free his people. From years of counseling men and women, Dr. Breuninger has a keen sense of what binds people and how the bondage and their woundedness prohibit them from living fully human lives.

In one way or another, all of us are wounded and in need of grace and healing. Dr. Breuninger provides a model for the reader that leads us to a place of freedom and wholeness. Our woundedness, no matter how great, does not have to be a barrier to living a life of freedom. Dr. Breuninger points out that we are often aware of our bondage due to being broken, but we don't know what to do to become free. Oftentimes, our best efforts actually make things worse. It's ultimately only through the grace and power of God that the freedom, the healing he has for us, is manifested in our lives. Dr. Breuninger leads us to an encounter with Jesus so we may experience the freedom He has won for us.

FR. DAVE PIVONKA, TOR
President, Franciscan University of Steubenville

INTRODUCTION

EACH SUMMER OUR TOWN hosts a track club for local children. Any child ages five to eighteen can participate. During the track meets, while each age group runs, the other kids wait on the grass field inside the track. While some of the older kids ran, I watched the five- and six-year-olds on the field. God bless their coach. It looked like she was herding cats. But as I watched, something struck me—those kids looked free. They ran around, jumped, twirled, rolled, poked each other, all with great freedom. They didn't seem afraid, worried about who was watching, or concerned with impressing each other. Even more, their motivation was innocent. They didn't seem self-interested or self-centered. They interacted with one another in an authentic and sincere (albeit sometimes chaotic) way. After one practice my five-year-old son even came up to me and said, "Dad, I told my team, 'If one of us wins, we all win!'" His excitement and sincerity were tangible. As I watched those little kids, I felt envious. I felt envious of their innocent freedom. They lived with the passion and openness of David dancing before the ark of the covenant. They were free.

I've tasted some of that freedom, but there was a time in my life when I felt crushed by the weight of my emotional pain. One night, at the age of nineteen, I found myself driving down the street, crying, gripped by the desire to end my life. It was the first time that my desire to die was greater than my fear—and that really scared me. At that point, I was living with significant anxiety, depression, resentment, and a sense of meaninglessness. I had significant emotional suffering and pain that I didn't know what to do with. My best attempts at reducing my discomfort only seemed to cause more problems. So, I put myself at the mercy of some selfless individuals who reintroduced me to God and a pattern of living that allows me, when I practice it in all of my daily experiences, to experience reasonable happiness, peace, and sense of purpose. This book is about freedom. It's my attempt to share some of the wisdom and concrete steps to healing that have allowed me to taste freedom.

Many of us explicitly believe or at least have a strong intuition that Jesus, through His Mystical Body, the Catholic Church, and in the sacraments, has the power to heal us. We often trust that He wants to heal us. We've heard in the Scriptures in both the New and Old Testaments that He desires to comfort us in our pain and bind our wounds. We deeply desire this healing.

It is not uncommon, however, that we experience no meaningful or substantial healing when we bring our pain and suffering to Christ in prayer and Confession, or when we lay them before His love in the Eucharist. We're left feeling disheartened, confused, or worse, abandoned. Therefore, this book seeks to help anyone who is suffering emotionally—anyone who is wounded—to encounter Christ in such a way that they can experience and receive the healing He desires for them.

The Key to Our Problems: Ourselves

Thankfully, much of our psychological and emotional suffering can be traced back to sources over which we have control. The real problem seldom *completely* lies outside of us. It may feel like the problem is my spouse, significant other, boss, friends,

Introduction

parents, job, school, or finances. But often, the problem is *me*. I need to learn how to recognize my excessive desire for security and identify the protective strategies I've developed to avoid suffering and pain—protective strategies that allow me to feel in control and secure. These security-seeking activities in all their manifestations (e.g., overachievement, procrastinating, acting in rage, playing the victim, greed, vainglory, manipulating my environment and those in it to get what I want or what I think I need) all block me from the healing touch of Christ in the sacraments, impeding my ability to hear His voice and do His will.

Now, this is not to say that the suffering caused by our friends, spouses, parents, and bosses is not real. We really do experience hurt by them. That hurt is real. Suffering like this is, unfortunately, inescapable in a fallen world. Everyone is hurt. I am not dismissing or diminishing this hurt. In fact, a sign of a healthy individual is the ability to experience the appropriate feelings—feelings like anxiety, sadness, loneliness, and anger—to the right degree, in the right circumstances. We should be deeply saddened by the death of a parent, by the end of a (healthy) romantic relationship, and by the divorce of parents. Someone who has been the victim of sexual assault or bullying *should* feel angry, sad, betrayed, and scared. Genuine emotional health allows us to acknowledge and experience suffering, while still retaining the freedom to pursue God's voice, His call, and His will for us in any given moment.

Chronic and/or debilitating emotional experiences often arise, at least in part, because we increase and extend the natural suffering that accompanies an experience by trying to avoid further suffering. The protective, safeguarding behaviors that we adopt to avoid suffering or perceived threats to our safety contribute to our persistent and painful distress. By living for security we are not free. We are slaves to our pain and suffering; they control us. We're compelled to orchestrate

Introduction

our lives in ways that reduce our pain and increase our security. If God's call on our life may result in some suffering, we can't follow it in freedom. We must react to our suffering.

To find deep meaning, peace, and contentment, we must follow Christ. We all know this. Christ says to His disciples, "If any man would come after me, let him deny himself and take up his cross and follow me. For whoever would save his life will lose it, and whoever loses his life for my sake will find it" (Matt 16:24–25).

Our happiness is found in following the Lord. Most of us assume that this simply means that we must follow His commandments. Obeying the Lord's commandments is certainly essential to following Him, but there's more! In our call to follow Christ, we are invited to trust Him—to trust that He will care for us and provide what we need to follow Him. Yet, many of us step out in front of the Lord to control and orchestrate life in ways that we think will provide a sense of security precisely because we don't trust Him. Not really. We don't trust that by following Christ we will experience security. We believe that we must seek our own security before we can really follow Him. We have to save ourselves. "I'll follow you Jesus, as soon as I've achieved the kind of security I need!"

In stepping out in front of Christ, we cause problems and undermine the very security we desire. We want to feel secure—to avoid suffering and pain—so we essentially say, "Lord, I've got this." This is how we fail to deny ourselves. An aspect of denying ourselves is letting go of all of the ways that we prioritize our desires for excessive security and self-preservation, rather than following the Lord. When the Lord says, "Whoever would save his life will lose it," He means, at least in part, that as we grasp at creating the life *we* want through our methods of self-preservation, we cut ourselves off from the living, giving Spirit.

Introduction

Sometimes, false beliefs drive our emotional difficulties. For example, rather than merely feeling the uncomfortable and unpleasant emotions of anger, sadness, and regret associated with losing a healthy romantic relationship, we develop false beliefs about ourselves and others (e.g., I'm not lovable; I can't handle the sadness of losing a relationship again; I need to know that a relationship will last before I can be vulnerable; others can't be trusted). These beliefs add anxiety, defensiveness, loneliness, and despair to the suffering already associated with the breakup. These false beliefs add to the intensity of the suffering and can serve as a barrier to healing, prolonging the emotional pain. Further, our false beliefs often cause us to act and react in ways that bother others, prompting them to respond to us in ways that we do not like, further hurting us. Christ tells us, "I am the way, and the truth, and the life" (John 14:6). We must encounter Christ, the Truth, to purify us of the false beliefs about ourselves, others, and the world. We need to meet Christ in a new and profound way so that He can reveal the truth of ourselves to us.

Suffering vs. Pain

For the purposes of this book, I will distinguish between suffering and pain. This is not a universal distinction. That is, not everyone thinks about these two words as distinct in this way. Many people use the words interchangeably. I've found, however, that it can be helpful to distinguish between the two to make sense of our experiences more fully. So, in this text, when I speak of suffering, I am referring to the inevitable hurt that comes with living an authentically Christ-centered life. Suffering happens. We get hurt and wounded by life. Pain, on the other hand, is the distress and anguish that we add to our suffering. Pain is our contribution to suffering. We create pain when we trying to avoid suffering through various means of

Introduction

self-preservation. The tremendous mental and emotional distress we experience can often be removed, dramatically reduced, or transformed by grace through recognizing where our approach to suffering has added pain.

What This Book Is and Is Not

It's important to address from the outset what this book is and what this book is not. This book is not the definitive text on emotional and psychological healing. Truthfully, there is no definitive text on emotional and psychological healing. If there were, then there wouldn't be an estimated five hundred unique therapies.[1] Despite what some people might say or how convincingly they might sell their story, no one method or model of healing works for everyone. In the field of psychotherapy, research on the effectiveness of different psychological treatments consistently shows little to no significant difference in the effectiveness of the various well-established treatments.[2] Most treatments are equally effective for most disorders. What researchers have found is that cutting across all of these treatments are a handful of common factors that contribute to healing.

So, do not fall for the lie when someone sells their method or approach as *the way*. The truth is some approaches resonate with certain individuals and help them make sense of their experience and get unstuck emotionally and psychologically. That is wonderful. The same approach may not work for someone else. Perhaps it's too intellectual, not intellectual

---

[1] Donald A. Eisner, *The Death of Psychotherapy: From Freud to Alien Abductions* (Westport, CT: Praeger Publishers, 2000).

[2] Bruce E. Wampold, Gregory W. Mondin, Marcia Moody, Frederick Stich, Kurt Benson, and Hyun-nie Ahn. "A Meta-Analysis of Outcome Studies Comparing Bona Fide Psychotherapies: Empirically, 'All Must Have Prizes.,'" *Psychological Bulletin* 122, no. 3 (1997): 203.

Introduction

enough, doesn't emphasize the mercy of God enough, or discusses God too much before the person is ready. Regardless of the reason, it's perfectly okay if an approach doesn't work for someone. This book is simply intended to be an aid. It provides one way, though certainly not the only way, of thinking about your problems. It is a way that interfaces with the Catholic faith and opens the healing process up to the grace of God. This method will not resonate with everyone and that is just fine. If you are not receiving any benefit from this approach, then simply put the book down and continue to explore other approaches to emotional and psychological healing that resonate with you. This book only seeks to be of service. It claims to be nothing more than a distillation of wisdom, approaches, and treatments that have worked for some in the past. If you are one of the individuals with whom this book does not resonate, that is just fine. There is nothing wrong with you. Emotional and psychological healing is not a one-size-fits-all experience.

Further, while I believe this book will be of great benefit to many, it is not intended to be a replacement or a substitution for therapy, medication, or spiritual direction. There are those whose emotional and psychological pain should be monitored and treated by a mental health professional. Even people afflicted with mental illnesses or psychological disturbances that required the help of a mental health professional should be able to benefit greatly from this book because when we are in the swirling storm of emotional suffering, we can either adopt ways of thinking and acting that increase our distress or foster ways of thinking and acting that will reduce the likelihood that we will contribute more pain to an already difficult situation. Further, this book can also help those with diagnosed mental illnesses to appreciate that the suffering they are enduring can be approached in a way that gives life meaning and purpose. That is, without compounding their suffering with more pain, they can recognize how God uses them and their suffering to serve Him in establishing the kingdom of heaven.

While this book is not intended to replace psychotherapy, medication, or spiritual direction, it can function as an aid *to all* who may be suffering. Some individuals may choose to use this book as a standalone resource, following its simple steps on their own. Others may choose to use the instructions in this book in conjunction with psychotherapy or spiritual direction. Either should be fine.

This book is intended to reveal you to yourself, to show you where you are adding pain to the sufferings of life. I will give you a framework and language to help you see the ways that you are a slave to self-protection. In seeing the pain you bring to your life, you will be given a chance to live in a radically different manner—a way of life that is more authentic, useful, and contented.

A Total Commitment

There is one last important point about this book that I hope readers will take to heart: The process of healing that I am proposing in this book is not for the faint of heart. It will be required of you to face, examine, and explore difficult and painful memories and experiences that have caused or been related to great suffering in your life. I do not recommend starting to read this book unless you are ready and willing to do whatever is recommended to you in the service of healing. This book is not merely an intellectual exercise, but rather lays out a pattern of living to follow daily to foster and establish a sense of peace and healing in your life. The practical steps laid out in this book require real work. You'll be asked to write certain things down, share certain experiences with others, and try to pass on the experience of healing to those who

Introduction

might be in pain. Taking *action* will be an essential step in the healing process. If you are not ready to take action, that is, deliberate, concrete steps to begin and maintain the healing process, then now may not be the best time to begin reading this book.

What I propose in this book as a path to healing will require an openness and willingness to change your entire life. You will be asked to lay everything on the table—your habits, ideas, goals, character traits, and friendships—scrutinizing them under the light and love of the Lord. You will be asked to surrender, change, and be transformed. I struggle with laziness. When there is an easier path, I find it and take it! I love when my doctor tells me there is a pill or medicine for a problem. I hate when he says the solution is diet and exercise. Well, this program is akin to the diet and exercise of healing. There is no pill or easy path. It will require hard work and substantial change on your part.

Perhaps like many of us, you're on the fence. You have an intense desire to experience healing, but you find yourself afraid that the process of healing might overwhelm you—might crush or destroy what is left of you. I can relate to that feeling. I can also relate to the fear—what if I do all this work and I'm still not any better? If this is the case, then it is my sincere prayer and desire that you read on, for it is the merciful love of God that will provide the courage and motivation to go to those dark places that you fear the most, if you simply present Him your willingness.

If all of this sounds curious or foreign, I get it. It is a new way of thinking and living that takes some getting used to. I will do my best to explain the idea thoroughly in this book. The first five chapters of the book are longer chapters. Because some of these concepts may be new to you, I repeat ideas in various ways throughout the book. I also use numerous metaphors and examples to try to illuminate the ideas. In these

Introduction

chapters I discuss our propensity to pretend that we're not hurting, our need to admit that we are struggling, the how and why of becoming wounded, different types of wounds, and how our response to our wounds becomes the very cause of our inability to heal. These chapters lay the rationale and groundwork for the six-step pattern for living detailed in the next three chapters. Each of these three chapters is short, containing practical, action-oriented explanations of two steps. These chapters are intended to be blueprints for how to work the steps and begin your path of healing.

When I was nineteen years old, I was introduced to a set of steps and a pattern of living like the one I am laying out before you. It changed my life. I have met some of the most amazing people, traveled to fantastic places, and experienced what it is to be of genuine service to God and to man. I have also suffered during that time. But, to the extent that I come back to these basic principles for living, I have a power to get through the sufferings of my life. If you choose to embark on this journey, know of my prayers for you. You are brave. Rest in the truth that we serve the King of kings and the Lord of lords, though. There is nothing that His love cannot transform.

Chapter 1

EVERYONE SUFFERS

I see the Church as a field hospital after battle. It is useless to ask a seriously injured person if he has high cholesterol and about the level of his blood sugars! You have to heal his wounds. Then we can talk about everything else. Heal the wounds, heal the wounds.
—*Pope Francis*[1]

EVERYONE SUFFERS. EVERYONE. This is a great and undeniable truth of our human condition. When I speak of suffering in this book, I'm not referring primarily to physical suffering (though we all suffer to some extent physically as well); I am talking about interior suffering—emotional and psychological suffering. Certainly, this kind of psychological anguish can often follow physical suffering and can even cause it in some cases, but emotional suffering is deeply distressing in its own right. Let me say it again. We all suffer. We all experience distressing memories, negative thoughts and feelings,

---

[1] Quoted in Antonio Spadaro, SJ, "A Big Heart Open to God: An Interview with Pope Francis," *America Magazine*, September 30, 2013, https://www.americamagazine.org/faith/2013/09/30/big-heart-open-god-interview-pope-francis.

and unwanted emotions like anger, anxiety, sadness, and loneliness. We carry within us the wounds of our experiences, which cause us significant distress and discomfort. Most people spend significant energy and effort to push these unpleasant experiences, memories, and feelings out of their minds, to keep them at bay. After all, our interior distress often feels overwhelming and unconquerable. But we're not alone in our hurt.

The Blessed Mother—conceived without sin, the perfect human being—experienced profound interior suffering. That is why we honor her under the title Our Lady of Sorrows. Mary endured tremendous interior anguish. Remember the prophecy by Simeon that a sword would pierce her heart (Luke 2:35)? Imagine the stress and anxiety she felt as she left home and fled to a foreign land with her newborn for fear that He would be killed. I'll never forget how incredibly stressed I felt to pack up our home in Houston and move to Ohio with an eight-week-old baby (and, I might add, no one was trying to kill our child for fear he might be the Messiah!). How must Mary have suffered when Jesus was lost for three days? The fear and worry; the sleepless nights; the confusion and self-doubt. "How could I lose the Son of God!" Of all the sufferings Mary endured, however, none was so great as the Passion of her Son. Mary must have felt such righteous anger, grief, horror, and loneliness as she watched her Son be mocked, tortured, and crucified. Mary knew suffering.

Even Our Lord suffered emotionally in His sacred humanity. The Book of Isaiah refers to the coming Messiah as "a man of sorrows" (Isa 53:3). The suffering servant. His suffering goes beyond the physical pain of the Cross. Our Lord suffers interiorly. Imagine how Jesus must have felt about the wayward children of Israel when He wept over the city of Jerusalem (Luke 19:41–44). Sadness gripped Him, like a parent whose child has lost their way in life. Just as a parent, carrying the burden of love, aches to the very core for their hurting children, so too did Our Lord hurt for the people of Jerusalem, who turned their back on the Father and turned the Temple into a marketplace. Again, we see the Lord's suffering and sadness in the death of His friend Lazarus. Jesus cries and, in doing so, aligns Himself with us, showing us that He knows the discomfort and hurt of loss. Finally, in His agony in the garden, Our Lord experiences such distress of soul, such emotional suffering, that He says that His soul is sorrowful "even to death" (Mark 14:34). His interior suffering was so great that He felt as if He could die right there and then!

As a Catholic psychologist, someone who understands the faith and is well acquainted with emotional suffering and distress, I'm amazed at how frequently I find myself thinking, "I can't believe *this* person needs help. I thought they had it all together. They always seem so happy." Don't get me wrong, I'm always happy when someone is willing to enter therapy. I certainly don't think that there's *any* shame in seeing a therapist or counselor (in fact, I think almost everyone should see a therapist at some point). My point is, sometimes *I* buy the lie that some people aren't suffering; that there are people who are exempt from the normal human experiences of emotional suffering.

I've had the privilege of accompanying clients from all walks of life in my therapy practice. On the surface, many of these individuals seem content and happy. They're wealthy, have large families, stable jobs, beautiful spouses, positions of privilege in the local community, and esteem in the Catholic community. When the office door closes, though, they share with me deep suffering, pain, sadness, feelings of self-doubt, self-loathing, suicidal thoughts, anxiety, and despair. As strange as it may sound, these experiences are always edifying because they remind me again—everyone suffers. No one is exempt.

The Universal Cover-Up

Perhaps that sounds strange. Why might I need to be reminded that everyone suffers? The answer is simple. Because most of us walk around acting like we are fine. We pretend. We pretend that we're not struggling with anger, anxiety, stress, depression, fear of not being good enough, fear of not getting what we want (the list goes on and on). We pretend that everything is okay. We present the mask of self-sufficiency to the world, projecting an image of contentment. Catholic philosopher and apologist Peter Kreeft calls this the "universal cover-up." We deny our emotional suffering and cover it with a veneer of "I'm doing just swell."

I remember one Easter when our young family was living in Houston. We were trying to get out the door for Easter Mass. If you know anything about Houston, you know that, curiously, no matter where you are in the city, you are always forty-five minutes from where you need to be. Naturally, this meant that we needed to get out the door not only early enough to make the long drive but also early enough to beat the crowds and find a seat for the family. My wife and I struggled to get all of the kids wrangled up and dressed (and to keep them dressed while we got ready). It was stressful and frustrating. "We gotta go or we aren't going to get a seat!" I yelled through the house. As we stumbled out the door, already running late, my wife said, "Oh, let's get an Easter picture in front of the tree." Realizing that it was futile to argue with my very pregnant wife, I said, "Okay, but let's hurry," and set the iPhone precariously on the window of the van as she started to organize the kids. I set the auto-timer for ten seconds, ran into the picture, and FLASH! I ran back and checked the picture and of course one of our children's eyes were closed, one child was not looking at the camera, and another child was making a silly face. "It's no good. The kids aren't looking at the camera. Oh well. Get in," I said. But my wife, committed to getting a good picture,

Everyone Suffers

insisted we do another one. By now, you might imagine, I am feeling utterly beat down from all of the energy it took to get three children in their Easter outfits. I'm also feeling frustrated at the kids for not holding still for the photo. I'm feeling angry at my wife for insisting on a picture before Mass, rather than waiting until after. I'm also feeling guilty for being angry at my pregnant wife. And, to top it all off, I'm feeling anxious that we aren't going to get a seat at Mass and that my about-to-have-a-baby-at-any-moment wife and I will be left standing and holding children. After two more attempts, the stars aligned and for a brief moment in time everyone was looking at the camera, smiling. It really was a stunning photo. I hurriedly ushered everyone into the car and on the ride over to Mass my wife uploaded the picture to Facebook.

When we came out of Mass, I was scrolling Facebook and noticed that the picture had something like two hundred-plus likes from our friends and family. I couldn't help but chuckle. I imagine that many who saw the photo thought to themselves "Wow, the Breuningers are such a delightful family. All the kids are so well dressed; everyone is happy and smiling; they have it all together." You would have been dead wrong! I felt so stressed and frustrated at the time of that picture. The point is, I'm sure some people compared how they were feeling on the inside that Easter morning, as they struggled to get their families ready or ached with loneliness or fought back anxiety and despair, to how the Breuningers looked on the outside. While social media has made this process easier, it's certainly not a new phenomenon. We look at the masks and images projected by those around us and we feel like we're the only ones who aren't happy, joyous, and free. Like we're the only ones not loving every minute of life.

Reasons We Pretend

If we are all hurting so badly, why are we all pretending that we aren't? Why don't we admit to one another that we are struggling and suffering from these unpleasant and distressing thoughts, feelings, and memories?

One reason we do not admit our suffering is not so much about pretending as it is about ignorance of our suffering. Some people are so used to chaos and unhappiness that they become accustomed to it. It's their normal. It feels like their baseline state. To them, it's simply the way things are and there's no other way to be. But when happiness and freedom are placed before many of these individuals, they are capable of realizing just how much they were suffering. Relatedly, some people know that they are experiencing some sort of emotional and psychological suffering, but they do not have the language or words to put to their experience. The experience almost seems to escape them because they don't have the terms or categories to discuss their experience. I've worked with numerous veterans who can only identify the feeling of anger. Working with them requires giving them names and words so that they can understand and appreciate their experiences more fully.

Some folks pretend that they are not suffering because they feel as if there is nothing they can do about their situation. They feel helpless and hopeless. There seems to be no solution to their problems. So many of these individuals try to push their unhappiness out of their minds, shoving their emotional suffering out of sight because there doesn't seem to be an answer. Why dwell on our pain and suffering if we'll only feel worse knowing that we are stuck in it?

One of the most common reasons that we put on the happiness mask, however, is because of our deep fear that if people saw our struggles and emotional wounds, then they would abandon us. See, we've been made for connection and communion with others. It's embedded deep in our DNA; it's rooted in our creation in the image of a God who is a communion of persons. We hear of this deep desire for connection with others as Adam exclaims, "This at last is bone of my bones and flesh of my flesh" (Gen 2:23), Adam is saying, "Finally, someone I can have communion with!" It's an exclamation that reveals our fundamental need for relationships with other people. The problem is, while we want connection and communion, while we desire to be seen and known deeply by others, we are also terrified that if we share certain unfavorable, unacceptable, or "bad" parts with others, then they will leave us. This is called the central relational paradox. We are constantly balancing our desire to be known and connected with our fear that being truly known will mean being abandoned. So, many of us hide those parts of ourselves that we deem bad or unacceptable. We keep those parts of ourselves out of connection and communion with others.

Adding to this fear of being abandoned by others, many of us in the Church pretend that we are not suffering because to do so would make us feel like failures. We believe that the Church is a place of healing. We believe that the sacraments, especially the Eucharist and Confession—the sacraments of love and forgiveness—should be able to heal our broken hearts, quiet our anxious minds, relieve our stress, and comfort our disappointment. We believe that the sacraments have the power to make us well. After years and years of faithfully bringing our suffering, pain and hurts, habitual sins, and difficulties to the sacraments, however, many people feel no better. They are no more patient, and no less gripped by lust, plagued by depression and anxiety, burdened with insecurity and fear, tormented with self-doubt and self-pity, and filled with anger and stress. We believe that Christ has the power to heal, in fact, we say it every Sunday: "Lord I am not worthy that you should enter under my roof, but only say the word and my soul shall be healed." Since we are not any better off, we assume that the problem must be us. We must be doing something wrong. We must be misunderstanding something. We don't admit the depth of our struggling with those in our Church because what might that mean about us? When we look across the pews, we see other families whose problems and sufferings seem to be so small, so manageable, so quaint, while our emotional suffering looks and feels huge. Rather than acknowledge our lingering and lasting suffering, we pretend (for others) that we have received healing and peace in those areas in our life in which we are still struggling.

Finally, many of us pretend that all is well, denying the real depths of our emotional suffering because to admit suffering would mean that we might need to change. That is, if we acknowledge that something is wrong, we might have to do something about it. And this can often be scary for a few reasons. First, to change means to give up our security and embrace vulnerability. Very often the patterns of thinking and habits that are causing so many of our emotional problems have been adopted over the years to keep us safe and secure. We've learned and practiced these habits as ways of trying to get our needs met. To admit our suffering means that we might have to address these habits, which means that we might leave ourselves feeling vulnerable, exposed, and insecure. Why would we willingly give up the strategies we've developed to achieve a sense of security? After all, they may not be perfect, but they provide us with at least a little, small sense of security. We're comfortable with our thought patterns and habits, even if they cause us to suffer. We've become so accustomed and familiar with them that, for many of us, they feel like a part of our personality. "I'm just sarcastic. It's who I am." "I just like things a certain way. Neat and organized. Always have." "I'm just the talkative one." "People just gravitate toward me and tell me their problems." To change would feel like we are giving up some part of ourselves.

Change Is Difficult

Admitting that we need change can also kick up fear regarding the hard work that change demands. Many of us sense that the process of growing and changing is a long and arduous journey. Flannery O'Connor summarized it well when she wrote, "All human nature vigorously resists grace because grace changes us and the change is painful."[2] While we may be unhappy and displeased with the way life is now, changing would likely take so much effort, energy, and struggle that unless we can be guaranteed a significant improvement and increase in happiness, we are not willing to make the effort.

We're right to assume that changing will be a hard process. C. S. Lewis masterfully brings to life how uncomfortable healing can be in his book *The Great Divorce*.[3] A poignant encounter occurs between a man with talkative lizard grafted onto his shoulder and an angel who wants to heal him. Now, in the story, the lizard represents the vice of lust, but the story has a broader application. It illustrates our fear of changing in general. The lizard constantly chitters and chatters in the man's ear. He feels frustrated and annoyed by the lizard's persistent talking. When the angel offers to remove the lizard, however, the man hesitates as the angel raises its fiery hands. The man immediately becomes afraid, asking the angel whether taking the lizard will hurt. The angel affirms that it will hurt, but that the man will be better for it. The man's fear of discomfort prevents him from giving his consent to the angel to take the

---

[2] Flannery O'Connor, *The Habit of Being*, ed. Sally Fitzgerald (New York: Farrar, Straus and Giroux: 1979), 307.
[3] The following scene is taken from C. S. Lewis, *The Great Divorce* (New York: HarperCollins, 1946), 99–106.

lizard. How often is this true of us? Our fear of discomfort prevents us from doing the necessary work to heal our emotional suffering. Further, not only is the man afraid of the discomfort, but he cannot imagine what his life will be like without the lizard. The little lizard has become a part of him. Though the lizard causes him much suffering, the man has become accustomed and comfortable with the consistent chattering in his ear. He struggles to conceive of what life might be like without this companion. It is familiar after all, and we are creatures who love familiarity. We like consistency.

The man in Lewis's story knows what to expect from his suffering, but what the angel offers him is uncertainty. The angel tells the man that he will be healed, but the man has never experienced this freedom. Are we not like the man with the lizard? We don't know what to expect from the process of healing other than discomfort. The thought of facing our demons without some assurance of what lies on the other side makes us wary to try. Even worse, what if after all of our hard work we don't feel any better?

So, we pretend. We remain stuck. But make no mistake, we are all wounded. We are all carrying hurts and emotional burdens that overwhelm us, embarrass us, and scare us. From the prince to the pauper, the pope to the parish priest, we all carry wounds that need healing. Pope Francis recognized this reality when he said in one of his homilies, "How many people need their wounds to be healed! . . . This is the Church's mission: healing the wounds of the heart, opening doors, liberating, and saying that God is good, God forgives all, that God is Father, that God is gentle, that God always waits for us."[4] If we are going to heal, we must first acknowledge that we are indeed wounded and hurting.

---

[4] Pope Francis, Homily at Santa Marta (February 5, 2015), https://www.vatican.va/content/francesco/en/cotidie/2015/documents/papa-francesco-cotidie_20150205_i-will-cure-you.html.

Everyone Suffers

Questions for Reflection

1. In what areas of life are you experiencing stress, unhappiness, anger, fear, or dissatisfaction? Are there relationships, jobs, vocational commitments, or other responsibilities that feel overwhelming or cause distress? What events or experiences from your past are still causing problems in your life today?
2. Take some time to reflect on why it's been so difficult to admit that you're suffering and struggling. What are the reasons that you've been pretending and covering up your struggles? What might happen if you stopped pretending?

Prayer

God, for so long I have been struggling and suffering, sometimes in big ways, sometimes in small ways, in so many areas of my life. I have not known what to do. I have not been able to fix the problems. I've been pretending that I am not hurting. I've been covering up my pain. I am tired of pretending and am exhausted from hiding my struggles. Grant me the humility to admit all of the wounds of the past that still bother me, and the willingness to acknowledge all of the current struggles that cause me frustration. Amen.

Chapter II
LOSE TO WIN

Jesus does not ask for glorious deeds. He asks only for self-surrender and for gratitude.

—St. Thérèse of Lisieux[1]

JOHN, A TWENTY-YEAR-OLD theology major, has been struggling with pornography and masturbation. Despite confessing this sin every few weeks for the past two years, the problem is not getting any better. Caroline, a twenty-four-year-old woman who was sexually abused during childhood, feels like she has forgiven the perpetrator, but still experiences anxiety in social situations, self-doubt and insecurity, panic attacks, and disordered eating. She receives the sacraments and has a vibrant faith, but her pain does not diminish. Frank is a successful, hardworking businessman in his mid-fifties. He is a devout family man, who has instilled the faith in his children and even has one son who entered the priesthood. Despite having a desire to love the Lord, praying a daily Rosary, and attending Mass regularly, he struggles with significant anxiety and depression. The list goes on and on.

---

[1] St. Thérèse, *The Story of A Soul: The Autobiography of St.Thérèse of Lisieux* (Charlotte, NC: TAN Classics, 2010), 158.

Over the years I've repeatedly witnessed genuine, well-catechized, faithful friends and colleagues, as well as priests and religious, receive the sacraments, pray novenas, say the Rosary, and remain just as broken, wounded, and hurting. They genuinely believe that the Church can heal their wounds and be a salve to their pain. Are they wrong? Is the Church not a place of healing?

The Church as a Place of Healing

In the Gospel of Luke, Jesus tells the parable of the Good Samaritan (Luke 10:25–37). In the parable, thieves attack a man traveling from Jerusalem to Jericho. The robbers beat him, take his clothes, and leave him badly wounded. A priest and a Levite, Jewish men of high standing, pass by the man leaving him for dead. It is only a Samaritan, a man hated by the Jews, who binds the traveler's wounds and takes him to an inn to care for him. Commenting on this parable, St. John Chrysostom writes,

> For the Inn is the Church, which receives travelers, who are tired with their journey through the world, and oppressed with the load of their sins; where the wearied traveler casting down the burden of his sins is relieved, and after being refreshed is restored with wholesome food. And this is what is here said, and took care of him. For without is everything that is conflicting, hurtful and evil, while within the Inn is contained all rest and health.[2]

---

[2] St. John Chrysostom, commenting on Luke 10:29–37, quoted in St. Thomas Aquinas, "The Catena Aurea, Gospel of Saint Luke," St. Isidore, accessed October 8, 2021, https://isidore.co/aquinas/english/CALuke.htm.

The early Church Fathers knew what the men and women I mentioned above know—the Church is a place of restoration of health and rest. It is a place of healing for the wounded! In his commentary on the Gospel of John, St. Augustine echoes this truth: "Let us be praying, as those who are wounded, for the physician; let us be carried into the inn to be healed."[3]

If the Church is in fact a place of healing for our wounds and alleviation of our suffering and pain, why do so many of us still greatly suffer from emotional distress—anxiety, anger, depression, gripping insecurity, and unhappy memories?

To our dismay, even when we bring these sufferings to our Lord in prayer, the sacraments, or religious devotions, we are left unhealed. We feel just as broken, wounded, and battered. How can we receive the Eucharist and bring ourselves to the graces of Confession Sunday after Sunday, year after year, and still be so wounded, still have our pain feel so fresh?

For many of us the problem is that we don't actually present the full extent of our hurts, wounds, and pain to Christ for healing. In order to be healed by Christ, to be restored to freedom, we must hand Him the depths of our pain—the full extent of our wounds. That is, we must let Him touch the rotten and sick parts of ourselves, the spiritual cancer that is at the root of our pain.

Deterrents to Healing: Lack of Self-Knowledge and Fear

What prevents us from giving Jesus the full extent of our problems? It seems to me that two things frequently serve as deterrents: lack of self-knowledge and fear. Oftentimes, we

---

[3] St. Augustine, *St. Augustine on St. John: Tractates, Homilies and Sermons on St. John's Gospel and First Epistle*, ed. Matt McCune (Morrisville, NC: Lulu Press, 2009), 283.

are not aware of the deep wounds and hurts that need to be healed by Christ. We confuse the effect of the wound with the wound itself—the fruit of the tree with the roots of the tree. We confess and lay before Christ our frustration and our anger. We offer Him our depression and anxiety. We tell Him all about our fights with our spouse, our sadness and frustration over our child who just won't listen, and all the ways people cause us to feel unhappy and uneasy. There is nothing wrong with sharing these difficult and painful situations with Christ, but we may be puzzled that we end up sharing the same situations and feelings over and over, week after week. If we're constantly sharing the same struggles with the Lord, it's likely because we are presenting Jesus the unpleasant fruits that arise from the deep wounds within ourselves that need to be healed. We should continue sharing these struggles, but unless we expose the roots and allow Him to take an ax to them, then we will not have lasting healing. The truth is, many of us don't know or appreciate our deepest wounds and motivations. Really knowing ourselves is crucial, for both healing and holiness. As St. Teresa of Ávila writes in her *Interior Castle*, "Self-knowledge is so important that, even if you were raised right up to the heavens, I should like you never to relax your cultivation of it."[4]

Alternatively, sometimes our inability to bring Christ into the depths of our woundedness and pain is the result of our fear of healing and changing. The change required for healing is painful and scary and will undoubtedly reveal many truths about ourselves—thoughts, habits, desires, and feelings—that may be difficult to admit and troubling to swallow. We'll begin to see how we play a significant role in much of our own pain. Healing demands that we must not only hand Christ the bad

---

[4] St. Teresa of Ávila, *Interior Castle*, trans. and ed. Edgar Allison Peers (Garden City, NY: Image Books, 2004), 14.

fruit that arises from our wounds, but we must dig into the depths of our hearts and expose the rotten roots. *Rotten roots bear bad fruits.* We need to allow Christ into deepest parts of ourselves that need healing so that He might touch them with His tender love.

Surrender to Win

In order to do this, we must first admit that we are in fact suffering. We must put up the white flag of surrender. We must admit to our innermost selves that we are in emotional pain and that our strategies for dealing with our pain and frustration are no longer working. We must concede that our strategies for managing our feelings and experiences are not as successful as we'd like. We must admit that we are not able to successfully combat feeling unloved and underappreciated by our parents, hating our bodies, feeling like a bad sexual partner, disliking our jobs, constantly overthinking everything, feeling annoyed and frustrated at our coworkers. Most of us are willing to invite God into certain areas of our life, but God wants all of our life—without reserve! Have we invited God into our anger, fear, sexuality, eating and drinking habits, our friendships, our marriage, and our jobs?

Jacob and Resistance to Surrender

In the Book of Genesis, we read the story of Jacob and Esau (Gen 25:24–34). Jacob was born on the heels of Esau, literally! The Scriptures tell us that Jacob grasped at Esau's foot as he was born. The name Jacob even means "to grasp at the heel," an expression in Hebrew that suggests deception. Jacob's name speaks of his character—he is a deceiver. Esau was born first, however, and as a result, received all of the birthrights associated with being the firstborn son. But Jacob uses deception and duplicitousness to achieve the happiness and security he desires. First, he convinces a hungry Esau to sell his birthright for a bowl of stew. If that wasn't bad enough, when the time arrives for Esau to receive his blessing from Isaac, their dying father, Jacob disguises himself as his brother and receives the blessing of the firstborn.

After years of separation, the two brothers prepare to meet. On his way to the meeting, Jacob, the deceptive man, famously wrestles with a divine being (Gen 32:22–28). Something curious happens, though. During the course of wrestling, despite being seemingly defeated, the divine being asks Jacob his name. In the ancient world, knowing someone's name gave you a certain power over them because one's name cut to the very reality of the person. Jacob gives this divine being his name. We can read into this action that Jacob surrenders to the divine being. He gives himself, the entirety of his being, and reality (symbolized by his name) over to the divine being. When he does this, his name and character—Jacob, the deceptive one—are transformed. He is given a new name and a new character, Israel. Jacob surrenders entirely and as a result he's transformed. He surrenders to win.

How often do we, like Jacob, wrestle with God before surrendering? How often do we subtly fall into self-reliance in so many areas of our life?

Fr. Walter Ciszek, the American Jesuit who spent more than a decade in Soviet prison camps, writes insightfully about how the "primacy of self" infiltrates our lives subtly, even in areas like prayer and evangelism. He cautions:

> For just as surely as man begins to trust in his own abilities, so surely he has taken the first step on the road to ultimate failure. And the greatest grace God can give such a man is to send him a trial he cannot

bear with his own powers—and then sustain him with his grace so he may endure to the end and be saved.[5]

It is not that God does not want us to acknowledge the gifts, talents, and abilities that He has given us. Or, that we should not use them. Rather, our problems arise when we trust our own abilities and powers to construct life and its circumstances, situations, and relationships as *we desire them to be.*

What Is Surrender?

To surrender is to give up control and self-sufficiency. It is to say, "I do not know the best way to act or the right way to think about this situation, relationship, or feeling." Surrendering acknowledges that my ways of managing my suffering and emotional pain are inadequate.

In our surrender, we "beat [our] swords into plowshares, and [our] spears into pruning hooks" (Isa 2:4). What does this mean? It means we lay down our arms, the defenses and coping strategies that we've deployed to fight off unwanted feelings and experiences, in order to find some peace. We place ourselves under God's command.

When an army surrenders, they lay down their weapons of defense and put themselves under the control of the other force. They stop fighting and do what they're told. They no longer presume to carry weapons or do whatever they want, but rather submit themselves to the actions and guidance of the opposing force. In our case, however, we surrender to God, not an opposing force—a God who loves us beyond measure.

Yet sometimes it can feel like we're surrendering to an opposing force. Why? Because often what God asks of us does

---

[5] Walter J. Ciszek and Daniel L. Flaherty, *He Leadeth Me: An Extraordinary Testament of Faith* (San Francisco: CA: Ignatius Press, 2006), 71.

not fall into line with what we would have chosen for ourselves. As Isaiah (55:8–9) tells us, "My thoughts are not your thoughts, neither are your ways my ways, says the LORD. For as the heavens are higher than the earth, so are my ways higher than your ways and my thoughts than your thoughts." God's action in our lives can feel jarring and contrary to what we desire, to the degree that our hearts are not already conformed to the Lord.

Willingness

What of willingness, though? The question of willingness is a separate but related question. While we may admit that our ways of thinking and acting have not been working as well as we'd like in various situations and relationships, we may be still unwilling to let God take over. We can admit defeat, but cannot submit to the Messiah. We're not yet willing to give God all access, so to speak, to the roots of our suffering. Unfortunately for us, this process requires that we hold nothing back. It requires that we be willing to expose the depths of all of our troubles.

Many of us work against the healing process precisely because we are unwilling to surrender all of our old attitudes, ideas, and habits. We haven't surrendered to the Lord what and how we think about parenting, discipline, politics, money, friendship, sex, food habits, right and wrong, good and bad, value, and identity. We hold on to some of these deep and unhealthy ideas and attitudes for fear that to give them up would mean that we might be giving up some of our security or identity. If you find yourself unwilling to surrender, unwilling to submit your attitudes, ideas, and behaviors to the scrutinizing light of the Lord, then you can pray for the willingness to be willing. An honest prayer is "God, give me the willingness to be willing to surrender all of myself to you."

An Example

A silly, but real, example to help illustrate: I have relatively high cholesterol and come from a long line of diabetics. My doctor has recommended that I change my diet. Unfortunately for me, I also have a tremendous sweet tooth and very little temperance when it comes to indulging in sweet treats. Most nights, I love to relax with my wife over a bowl of ice cream, a bag of peanut butter M&Ms, or some other snack. There's no balance in my life around this issue. I do big bowls and whole bags. Now, because I'm relatively skinny and look as if I'm in good shape, I don't feel a particular imperative to address the issue, yet. Historically, the lack of balance and moderation in this area of my life has been something that I am unwilling to consider or surrender. It's a bad habit that I accept because I'm not experiencing immediate consequences. My attitudes and ideas about a big nightly bowl of ice cream are "How will I relax at the end of a long day? I need a reward after working so hard; I need something for myself after giving to others all day." These are the roots of my habit and my frustration.

If I take an honest look at this habit, though, I realize that I'm afraid to surrender my attitudes, ideas, and habits to the Lord. I'm afraid to see what He might do to them. I recognize in myself an excessive desire for comfort and a fear that life might feel bland and boring without treating myself each evening. This fear is also a root cause of my habit and frustration.

In reality, despite the short-term benefits, this habit actually brings a fair amount frustration and discomfort—negative fruit. When my kids ask for ice cream for dessert or they ask for some of *my* M&Ms, I find myself frustrated and feeling stingy. I tell them they can only have one scoop of ice cream. After all, I need to make sure there is enough for me in the evening. Or I serve them a generous serving, but with a grumpy attitude, because they're jeopardizing what I perceive to be my bit of happiness for the day. Once I finally sit down to relax with my bowl, I become easily irritated if my kids need anything from me. "Don't they realize this is my time? That they're ruining my reward?" Not to mention, what if my cholesterol continues to rise or if I become pre-diabetic? Won't future health problems cause further unhappiness? I'll often complain to the Lord, "My kids just eat everything; my frustration is that they aren't grateful; I'm angry because they haven't learned to respect my relaxation." I'll give God the fruit, but rarely am I willing to dig into my own motivations or contributions to the situation. I don't put myself under the microscope to examine how my attitudes, ideas, and behaviors may be causing my problems.

Now, this is just a simple and silly example, but a real one. It illustrates the subtle ways we give ourselves passes and skirt our need to surrender all areas of our life, the fruit and the roots. I don't want to look at my frustration with my kids, my dessert habits, or the excessive fear and desire for comfort motivating them. I'm not yet in enough pain to warrant the discomfort and hassle of surrendering this area of my life to the Lord. We must surrender everything, though. St. Bernadette Soubirous reminds us, "Jesus gives all to those who surrender all."[6] If we want to be transformed, we must put down our defenses, our ways of coping and doing things, and surrender to God. We must admit that our approach and our way of doing this are simply not working for us.

We Can Do Nothing Apart from Him

Surrender means the willingness to put our lives under the microscope and examine whether we are operating from our

---

[6] Quoted in Patricia A. McEachern, *A Holy Life: St. Bernadette of Lourdes* (San Francisco: Ignatius Press, 2005).

power or God's power, our ways of doing things or God's. We submit every aspect of ourselves to the purifying light of God's love. Surrender is not just an idea, however. It is both an attitude and an action. As an attitude, surrender means we enter each day and each situation with the recognition that our way of thinking and acting may not be the best way. It's the acknowledgement that our approach might need to be changed. As an action, surrender means we actively and intentionally invite God into each situation. When we realize that we may not be approaching various situations in the healthiest ways, then we must be open to taking guidance from another; we must become receptive to the help and power of another. That one is God! Surrender means inviting God's power and guidance into each moment to direct us in whatever way He chooses!

Jesus says, "I am the vine, you are the branches. He who abides in me, and I in him, he it is that bears much fruit, for apart from me you can do nothing" (John 15:5).

These words of Christ should terrify us. Apart from Him, we can do nothing. Nothing! If we're honest with ourselves, we often attribute our accomplishments to our own power, recognizing God's contribution as relatively small (if any). Sure, we'll respond with a platitude ("Praise God!") when someone recognizes an accomplishment. In reality, though, we tend to think of ourselves as having achieved most of our daily accomplishments.

Yet, our unwillingness to surrender ourselves entirely—identity, thoughts, habits, feelings—to the Lord is merely an example of trying to live apart from the vine. We make ourselves the vine and convince ourselves that we will bear good fruit doing things our way. Christ is unflinching and clear: We will bear good fruit only if we are grafted into His life, allowing His power and grace to flow through every aspect of our lives. The truth is we must let go of the various ways that we have still not surrendered. We must identify the areas of our life where we are still operating from our attitudes, ideas, habits, and identities. We need to be willing to have all areas of our lives pruned so that we can be grafted to the Vine.

Questions for Reflection

1. In what ways are you living apart from the vine (i.e., the life and grace of Christ)? What areas of your life have you not yet brought God into? What parts of your life have not been surrendered to God? Why is it difficult to surrender here?

2. What do you think of and how do you feel when you imagine surrendering the entirety of your life (e.g., your relationships, all choices, career, plans, etc.) to God? What fears or anxieties arise for you when you consider surrendering your life to God?

3. Are you ready to surrender your ideas about what is most important, what you value, what you should be focusing on, and how you should be approaching various aspects of your life? If not, what is blocking you?

Prayer

Lord, I want to be totally Yours, but there are parts of my life that I still cling to. There are areas of my life that I want to be in control of. Please remove any fear of surrendering completely to You. Grant me the desire to turn my whole life over to You. I am told that in You I will find rest, peace, contentment, fulfillment, and happiness. Grant me the faith to believe that surrendering to You will bring me the happiness I desire—the life that I truly desire. Amen.

Chapter III

A GOD WHO WANTS TO HEAL

The hardness of God is kinder than the softness of men, and His compulsion is our liberation.

—C. S. Lewis[1]

WHEN JESUS ENCOUNTERED the sick man at the pool Beth-zatha, He put a question to him: "Do you want to be healed?" (John 5:6). Can you hear those words echoing throughout time to you? Right now, at this moment, Jesus still asks the same question of us: Do we want to be healed?

Jesus puts this question to the man precisely because He desires to heal him. Christ does not conform His will to the sick man's; rather, He questions the sick man in order to allow him to bring his will into conformity with God's. God wants to heal!

Original Sin and Its Consequences

We all suffer because we are all wounded. Our wounds occur when we fail to be loved the way we were created to be loved.

---

[1] C. S. Lewis, *Surprised by Joy: The Shape of My Early Life* (New York: Harcourt Brace & Co., 1955), 221.

The first, primordial wound from which we suffer is the disobedience of Adam and Eve. Before their disobedience, Adam and Eve enjoy deep love and harmony with nature, with one another, and with God. Through their disobedience, they rupture their unity with God. They cut themselves off from God's love. As a result, the harmony between themselves and their place within nature also become disintegrated. They are suddenly filled with fear and distrust: they hide from fear of God and cover their nakedness from each other in distrust.

The bad news is that we are all touched by this deep and primordial injury, a self-inflicted wound through which man killed the divine life within him. We continue to willingly wound ourselves in turning away from God, who perfectly loves us. Original sin really does harm man. It is a spiritual wound with physical and emotional consequences. We are created to have intimate union and communion with God, a free exchange of love and divine life. We are created to flourish. Original sin radically disrupts the union with God for which we are created and which is absolutely necessary for man to truly experience peace and flourishing.

The consequences of that original wound cut to the very heart of humanity, passing on from generation to generation. Two of the obvious consequences of the Fall are our darkened intellects and weakened wills. Our darkened intellect prevents us from accurately perceiving the truth. We're prone to seeing the world through distorted lenses, that is, through our hurts, fears, and selfishness, rather than through the truth of the situation and God's love. When we perceive the world through these distorted lenses, we tend to deepen our own hurts and fracture our relationships with others. Even when we know the truth, however, our will is still weakened. We still struggle to do the right thing. St. Paul says, "I can will what is right, but I cannot do it" (Rom 7:18).

We're all familiar with this twofold effect of original sin.

Think for a moment about those pernicious falsehoods that you tell yourself, which give rise to so much pain in your life: lies such as "I'm not lovable; nobody could ever find me attractive; I'm not good enough; I'm helpless; I'm not important or valued by anyone. I'm too broken." The list goes on. Along with these lies, think, then, about all of the ways we fail to choose what is good. We choose impatience, even when we know patience and perseverance are the right course of action. We choose to numb ourselves with TV, food, drink, and social media rather than feed ourselves with prayer. We choose to rationalize and intellectualize our bad behavior rather than admit fault and be honest. Much of therapy is spent trying to correct the falsehoods folks believe and help them choose actions that are in conformity with the truth.

The Good News: God Wants to Heal Us!

The bad news is that we're all touched by sin, but the good news is that we have a God who wants to heal us! Even after Adam and Eve's disobedience, their self-inflicted wound, God tells them that He wants to heal this wound. He says, "I will put enmity between you and the woman, and between your seed and her seed; he shall bruise your head, and you shall bruise his heel" (Gen 3:15). Scripture scholars call this the proto-evangelium—the first Gospel. And, since "gospel" means "good news," the proto-evangelium is the first good news—the good news that God wants to, and will, heal our wounds by giving us victory over sin. Notice that in His declaration, God, just like a loving Father, gives Adam and Eve this message of healing and hope first, before He shares the consequences for their disobedience (e.g., toiling over the land, pain in childbirth, etc.).

In His profound love for us, God willed that this first Gospel, this message of hope and healing, would literally take on our flesh and become human in the person of Jesus. The Book of Isaiah tells us of this suffering servant who will heal his people: "But he was wounded for our transgressions, he was bruised for our iniquities; upon him was the chastisement that made us whole, and with his stripes we are healed" (Isa 53:5). We are saved by Christ's death and Resurrection.

Jesus, Healer of Original Sin

The name "Jesus" means "the Lord is salvation." What is salvation, though? The root of the word "salvation" is the Latin word *salvus,* meaning "uninjured, in good health, safe." Salvation, therefore, is a restorative act by Christ through which He heals our wounds and returns us to safety and good health.

What does Christ heal? First, and most fundamentally, He heals the primordial injury of original sin. He binds and restores the broken union between man and God. He spiritually reunites man's soul with the divine life by the graces of His death and Resurrection made present to us in the sacraments. Baptism washes us clean from original sin with the healing graces of His death and resurrection.

Not Just Spiritual Healing

It's not uncommon that when we think about Christ's healing and salvation, we tend to think of them primarily as spiritual acts, which only concern the spiritual dimension of man. His healing however, is not merely spiritual. Jesus comes to heal everything related to original sin. He comes to bring complete salvation that not only addresses the spiritual, but also begins the process of healing the consequences of the Fall, our darkened intellect and weakened will.

A God Who Wants to Heal

The Incarnation educates our intellect. Through the Incarnation, Christ reveals to us the truth of who we are: "Christ, the final Adam, by the revelation of the mystery of the Father and His love, fully reveals man to man himself and makes his supreme calling clear."[2] In Christ, we are confronted with the truth of ourselves in a manner that we can see and touch. Our darkened intellect is given light! We are transformed by this light, and can now appropriate these truths. And there's more! Through the Incarnation, Christ also strengthens our will by giving us the grace to act in conformity with these truths. This healing may not reach full completion until heaven, but Christ offers it to each of us now!

The Gospel of John tells us, "God sent the Son into the world, not to condemn the world, but that the world might be saved through him" (John 3:17). God wants to save and to heal us, not in some distant mystical way, but tangibly, right now. He wants to touch the very depths and roots of original sin and begin to make order in our disorder, including the disorder of our emotional and psychological lives.

We see this truth powerfully exemplified in the story of the paralytic man, whose friends lower him through the roof to encounter Jesus. Upon seeing the man, Jesus's first action is to tell him that his sins are forgiven. This is significant, yet curious. Obviously, the man's most glaring problem is his paralysis. He has a physical ailment that needs healing. Jesus baffles and confounds the crowd by first forgiving the man's sins. By this action, Christ signifies that the deepest and most significant injury, our deepest and most significant wound, is our broken union with God. That is where healing must first occur. Only after forgiving the man's sins, and re-establishing

---

[2] Pope St. Paul VI, Pastoral Constitution on the Church in the Modern World *Gaudium et Spes* (December 7, 1965), §22.

the perfect union between God and man, does He heal the man's legs.

Healing the man's paralysis is not a separate or distinct act from the forgiveness of his sins. It is a healing grace which flows forth from his reconciliation with the Lord. Original sin caused disorder and disintegration in creation (e.g., disease), so the healing of original sin begins to bring about the restoration and healing of creation. St. John Paul II writes poignantly about this:

> The liberation and salvation brought by the kingdom of God come to the human person both in his physical and spiritual dimensions. Two gestures are characteristic of Jesus' mission: healing and forgiving. Jesus' many healings clearly show his great compassion in the face of human distress, but they also signify that in the kingdom there will no longer be sickness or suffering, and that his mission, from the very beginning, is meant to free people from these evils.[3]

Now, we should not expect that every act of reconciliation with God or forgiveness of sin will result in physical healing. Jesus comes to heal not only the spiritual roots of original sin but also the effects of original sin on creation, and this includes our psychological and emotional struggles. Considering the Incarnation in a weekly audience, Pope Benedict XVI echoed this sentiment:

> . . . reflecting on the Prologue to the Gospel according to St. John, in particular the sentence, "the Word

---

[3] Pope St. John Paul II, Encyclical on the Permanent Validity of the Church's Missionary Mandate *Redemptoris Missio* (December 7, 1990), §14.

became flesh." Here the word "flesh," according to the Hebrew usage, indicates *man in his whole self*, the whole man, but in particular in the dimension of his transience and his temporality, his poverty and his contingency. This was in order to tell us that the salvation brought by God, who became man in Jesus of Nazareth, affects man in his material reality and in whatever situation he may be. *God assumed the human condition to heal it from all that separates it from him*, to enable us to call him, in his Only-Begotten Son, by the name of "Abba, Father," and to truly be children of God.[4]

Benedict XVI reaffirms that the very purpose of the Incarnation is not the healing of everything that separates us God, including our attitudes, ideas, behaviors, and emotional pain, but also the reestablishment of a bond with the Father that allows us to address Him with childlike love and trust as "Abba."

Mistrusting the Goodness of God

Yet, we struggle to trust God. The *Catechism* tells us, "Man, tempted by the devil, let his trust in his Creator die in his heart and, abusing his freedom, disobeyed God's command. This is what man's first sin consisted of. All subsequent sin would be disobedience toward God and lack of trust in his goodness" (397). That idea should be jarring to us—our sins, both the ones we commit and the ones we perform by omission, flow from a lack of trust in God's goodness.

---

[4] Pope Benedict XVI, General Audience (January 9, 2013), https://www.vatican.va/content/benedict-xvi/en/audiences/2013/documents/hf_ben-xvi_aud_20130109.html; emphasis mine.

We struggle to trust that God is good and that He wants what's best for us. Does God really want what is good for me, we ask? My parents had a terrible marriage that ended in divorce; my dad was an alcoholic; my mother was emotionally abusive; I was sexually abused as a child or assaulted as an adult. If we look at the often painful circumstances of our lives, it can be very difficult to see how God desires our good. When we doubt God's love and care for us, we hold on to our own bids for happiness and security. We fall for the "monkey trap."

The story of the monkey trap goes like this: Various natives and aboriginals across cultures have learned to catch monkeys by cutting a hole in a gourd and hollowing it out. The hole is just large enough for a monkey to fit its hand. The gourd is placed on the ground with a few small rocks in it to weigh it down. Finally, the hunter places something the monkey desires—a piece of shiny tin foil, dates, fruit—into the gourd. Eventually, a monkey comes along and reaches into the gourd for the desired object. The catch is that the monkey can put their hand into the gourd's hole, but once the monkey makes a fist around the object, its hand becomes too large to get out of the hole. The monkey is stuck. Now, all the monkey has to do to get free is let go of the object. But it won't! A monkey will hold onto that object until the hunter comes to capture or kill it.

The story illustrates a phenomenon that we humans find ourselves in quite often. We grasp at desirable things in our lives even though they keep us trapped or ensnared. But why? Because we don't trust in God's goodness. We're afraid that maybe God is stingy. Maybe He won't look out for us. We'd best look out for ourselves. In living this way, we hold onto the very thoughts, ideas, habits, and behaviors that keep us trapped. We're afraid to let go because we don't trust God.

Why We Mistrust God: Attachment

Our view of God, the way that we've come to experience and perceive Our Lord, is related to our experiences with early childhood caregivers. We are born into a large, powerful, and overwhelming world, which we cannot navigate on our own. Therefore, we need to feel, in our very being, that our caregivers will keep us safe and protected. These caregivers, most often our parents, but sometimes a single parent, grandparent, or some other individual(s), are responsible for tending to our needs, both physical and emotional. If our caregivers meet our needs in a way that allows us to *feel* safe and secure, we develop what is called a secure attachment. The attachment bond is the social-emotional bond between a child and a caregiver.

Ultimately, attachment is about the degree of felt security that a child experiences in their interactions with a caregiver, an experience that eventually translates into a general sense of safety and security in one's own identity, a sense of being good enough, and emotional regulation. This feeling of security creates an emotional climate in which the child can explore their identity, make mistakes, experience big feelings, and learn how to regulate their emotions without fear of retribution—namely, the child can risk being human and ultimately flourish.

Attunement

For a parent to foster a secure attachment, three criteria must be met. They must interact with their child in an attuned, empathic, and consistent manner. When a parent is attuned to the needs of their child, it means that they accurately see what the child needs. Sometimes when my child is quiet, it's because they're tired and they need me to pick them up and rub their back. Sometimes when they're silent, it's because they're angry and they need me to empathize with their frustration. Sometimes when they're quiet, it's because they're scared, and they need me to provide a sense of safety and support. Being able to accurately see what my child needs communicates to them that they are worth knowing, worth paying attention to, that they are worth seeing. This isn't just an intellectual experience either: "I know Dad loves me." This is a felt experience. When somebody accurately sees what you need, you *feel* known, you *feel* seen. If a caregiver fails to see a child's needs, the child may avoid the caregiver and seek security on their own.

But simply seeing what's needed isn't enough.

Warmth

Once a caregiver can accurately identify the needs, they must then respond to those needs empathically—that is, with warmth. If my child is tired, or hungry or scared, and I respond to them in a compassionate manner, I signal that they shouldn't feel ashamed of their needs or be afraid of their experiences. I signal to them that it is okay to be as they are, and that I can understand why they feel the way they feel. Now, empathy doesn't mean I condone every action or experience of my child's. Sometimes when my kids act in an inappropriate manner, I provide correction or even a consequence, but I can still be empathic and show that I understand why my fourteen-year-old might've raised his voice at a younger sibling or why my five-year-old might've hit his little sister. I can show them that I really feel their frustration in my response to them, while still correcting their response in a situation.

The key when responding empathically is that I'm not severing the bond between myself and my child. I'm not communicating, "I will love you and reconnect with you once you change." An empathic response communicates that our relational bond is still intact. If we're having a difficult conversation, even if I am angry and frustrated with my child, I can respond to them in a way that acknowledges my anger and frustration, while simultaneously communicating that our bond and connection of love is still intact.

Unfortunately, some parents, when correcting their children or responding to their children's needs, may respond in a cold, distant, or disconnected manner. They may communicate a frustration that suggests they are disinterested in their child, or inconvenienced by the child's needs. Such responses, over time, diminish the child's felt security or sense of safety. A child in this situation may avoid their caregiver because the caregiver does not feel safe, or they might draw near to the caregiver but feel anxious in their presence.

Consistency

Finally, a parent must respond consistently. My children must know that time and again, to the best of my ability, I will respond to their needs accurately and empathically. See, we human beings despise uncertainty. When a child doesn't know whether their parent will respond with compassion or anger, empathically, or in a cold and distant manner, whether the parent will accurately see their needs or misread their needs, the child will feel anxious and insecure.

God Attachment

When these three ingredients are present to a sufficient degree, the child feels a sense of security or a secure attachment. Failure to provide these conditions adequately results in one of three types of insecure attachment. This attachment bond with caregivers serves as our template for our relationship to God. If we had a secure attachment to our caregivers, we likely have a secure attachment to God. An insecure attachment to caregivers means that we likely have an insecure attachment to God.

Interestingly, Adam and Eve had a deep sense of secure attachment to God in their original state of innocence. They were neither suspicious of God, nor did they feel afraid or worried about how He would react to them. All of their needs were met and they lived in a perpetual state of harmony with their divine caregiver, walking under His loving gaze and experiencing the warmth and consistency of His paternal care.

We see that once Adam and Eve eat of the tree of the knowledge of good and evil, insecure attachment enters the garden and Adam and Eve hide. They become afraid of God, not because of anything God has done, but because of their disobedience. They also become distrustful of God. A deep wedge is driven into man's heart, through which we struggle to believe that God is good. We become afraid that God does not desire what's best for us, that perhaps God is not attuned to us. This is what the *Catechism* speaks of.

So much of our struggle since the Fall can be traced back to trying to create and provide our own sense of security because we do not have a childlike trust in the goodness of our divine caregiver.

Doing Good and Healing

The Acts of the Apostles recalls Jesus as the man who went about "doing good and healing" (Acts 10:38). This is His character. It is His very nature because "God is love" (1 John 4:8). In his encyclical *Dives in Misericordia*, St. John Paul II writes, "Making the Father present as love and mercy is, in Christ's own consciousness, the fundamental touchstone of His

A God Who Wants to Heal

mission as the Messiah."[5] Christ is sent into the world to make known, in the flesh, in a way that can be seen and touched, the love and mercy of God.

In Christ's mission of mercy, we see an important link to healing. In His exposition of the virtue of mercy, St. Thomas Aquinas suggests that mercy makes itself known through the healing or remedy of misery. Misery, St. Thomas goes on to explain, is any sort of defect in a person. So, mercy results in the healing or remedy of a defect: "To feel sad about another's misery is no attribute of God, *but to drive it out is supremely His, and by misery here we mean any sort of defect*. Defects are not done away with save by an achievement of goodness, and as we have said, God is the first source of goodness."[6] Christ, as a divine Person, is this first source of goodness, which allows Him to drive out and heal our defects, our miseries. He is the man who goes around doing good and healing precisely because His mission is one of love and mercy.

The Love of a Father

I'm a decent father. I suspect I'm at the high end of average. I certainly have a far way to go and a lot of work to do to be a great father, but, even in my averageness, my love for my kids is strong and profound. I'll never forget one summer evening looking out into the backyard watching one of my kids toddle around. I felt like my heart was going to explode. My love for my child was so strong; it welled up so profoundly, that I felt as if my heart would come out of my chest. I love my children

---

[5] Pope St. John Paul II, Encyclical Rich in Mercy *Dives in Misericordia* (November 30, 1980), §3.
[6] St. Thomas Aquinas, *Summa Theologiae* 1.21.3, quoted in Dr. Robert Stackpole, "Saint Thomas Aquinas on Mercy Part 1," Marians of the Immaculate Conception, January 28, 2019, https://www.marian.org/news/The-Meaning-of-Mercy-3485; emphasis mine.

so much. It is this deep love for them that causes their hurt and wounds to pain me.

Once, during a family walk, I was pushing my young son in a little blue Fisher-Price car. At the top of the hill before our house, he said, "I run."

So, I said, "Okay."

He hopped out of his car and started running down the hill, his little legs going so fast—until, BAM! He fell face first. His legs couldn't keep up with his speed. I rushed down to him and scooped him up. My heart broke. He was in tears. He was trying so hard to explore his world, be a big boy, and in a mere instant, he went from flying to all scraped up. In the end, he was fine. He had a few scrapes on his knee—a normal part of every kid's childhood. But, as a parent, I found the moment difficult. Why? Because I love my child and I don't want to see him get hurt. I would do whatever possible to prevent his pain. I knew at that moment, however, the moment of his first scrapes, that the world would continue to hurt him and put scars on his perfect, unblemished skin. I knew what I wanted for him as a parent and I knew what life had in store for him. If this is how I, an average father, feel about my children, imagine how God the Father feels about His adopted children!

One thing that our Protestant brothers and sisters get right is their emphasis on the unmerited love of God. Sometimes, I get the sense that many of us in the Catholic world hold a subtle belief that we really do have to earn God's love. There is no way we could be loved unconditionally. There must be some catch. But alas, God is love! It cannot be said enough. It must sink into our very bones. It must repeat on our lips with every breath. He knows the plans He has for us. He knows what we were created for. To see us hurting, even when it's of our own device, grieves Him. The heart of the Father is merciful and tender. He is a Father who runs out to meet us, like the father in the parable of the prodigal son. He is not a passive father. He is a father who delights in us, loves us unconditionally, and asks us, "Do you want to be healed?" not because He does not want to heal us, but because He is desperate to. Since the Fall, it's predominated God's relationship with man—healing and restoration. No, He asks us that question so that we might cooperate with His healing.

God doesn't heal us in our way for our purposes. He heals us in His way for His loving purposes: "For I know the plans I have for you, says the LORD, plans for welfare and not for evil, to give you a future and a hope" (Jer 29:11).

If only we could trust Him.

He Can Handle Our Shame

To allow Christ to touch our defects, however, we often need to invite Him into some dark and often shameful places in our life. We need to allow Him to see those experiences, habits, and behaviors that we even try to hide from ourselves.

We are only as sick as our secrets.

We see this beautifully depicted in Jesus's encounter with the Samaritan woman. In the Scriptures, there is a common betrothal theme that occurs at wells. Just look at the story of Jacob, the namesake of the well where Jesus meets the Samaritan woman. Jacob meets his bride Rachel in this very place. Jacob's Well is where the betrothal between a bridegroom and a bride takes place. John's Gospel tells us that Jesus meets the woman at the sixth hour—that is, around noon. This is a strange detail, since most women would have gathered water early in the morning before the heat of the day set upon them. So, why was this woman at the well at that hour? Because she was ashamed. Here is a woman who has had multiple husbands and was currently living with a man who was not her husband. She is driven by shame. She does not have the interior freedom to go to the well with the other women, but rather goes alone in the heat of the day. Her secrets keep her sick. The well is not a place of life-giving water or love for her; it is a reminder of her shame. As she holds back her secrets, her shame grows and so does her isolation. She is a slave to her shame.

But she is called to freedom. She needs to be unburdened.

Christ is waiting for her at the well when she arrives. There is a sense of intentionality and anticipation in His presence. Jesus doesn't happen upon her in her place of shame; He is already there waiting for her. Unlike the burden of shame, His yoke is easy and His burden light. Jesus invites the woman to call her husband, to which the woman responds, "I have no husband" (John 4:17). Her response is an attempt to keep her secret, to hide her shame. She uses deceptive language to keep her secret hidden. Jesus, however, cuts to the very heart of her shame and tells her, "For you have had five husbands, and he whom you now have is not your husband" (John 4:18). Jesus brings her secret, the shame that has kept her enslaved, into the light. Christ calls out her hidden pain boldly and confidently. He's not afraid of her secret or of her shame. He wants it! He wants to set her free because that's the very reason for His coming into the world: He can give her the life-giving water that she desires.

How do we know that she is set free from her shame after her encounter with the Lord? Because she runs into the city to tell everyone that she has met the Messiah. The very people she wanted to avoid by going to the well at noon are the very people she now runs to, to share her news with. And in her willingness to approach them, to be in their midst, we see her freedom. She is liberated to share the good news.

A Final Note

Because we often view God as we view our parents, we struggle to trust Him. But I need you to hear this right now. Read this slowly and read it daily if you must: God is not waiting for you to be good enough to love. He loves you right now. He is a Father waiting to comfort you in all of your hurts; a Father wanting you to rest your head against His chest in your emotional exhaustion. He is a Father who is big enough to allow you to unburden all of your feelings; He's not afraid of them. He will not start loving you once you are better. He loves you now. He's not waiting for you to be perfect. You are beloved by God right now, in all of your shame, in all of the places that you feel most unlovable.

This Father sent the one whom He loved, His own Son, to die on the Cross to show you how very much He loves you. See, the Cross is our Jacob's Well. It is in the place that the Lord meets us in our shame. He does not wait until we're right, tight, and put together to love us. No! The Cross is Christ stepping into our secrets, our shame, our sin, and our pain and loving us there. He didn't die once we were perfect. He died to make us perfect. He goes to the Cross while we are in our sin and shame: "But God shows his love for us in that while we were yet sinners Christ died for us" (Rom 5:8). Let that sink in for a moment. It is free, gratuitous. It is not because you've done anything. You are loved, and not by a boring, static God, but by a God whose love is dynamic, passionate, real, and personal to you! God loves you and He wants to heal you—starting now and finding completion when you are finally back in the arms of your Father, seeing Him face-to-face.

Questions for Reflection

1. Do you believe, in the depths of your heart, that God wants to heal you? Do you believe that you can trust

the goodness of God? Write freely about what comes to you as you think about these questions.

2. When you think about turning to the Lord in your suffering and pain, what thoughts come to mind? What is your felt experience of God? When you turn to Him in your struggles, how do you feel? He do you think He feels about you when you are distressed or suffering?

Prayer

Abba, Father, give me the grace of experiencing Your unimaginable love for me. I want to be filled with trust in Your goodness and Your love as my Heavenly Father. I want to believe in the depths of my being that You are for me! That You want me! That You want me to be happy and free! Obliterate my old, untrue beliefs about You and replace them with the truth—that You are love. Help me to see You as You are. You do not think like my family members or friends—You are my Father and I am Your beloved. Place that truth deep within my heart. Amen.

Chapter IV

A BIT ABOUT WOUNDS

We have been created in his image. We have been created to love and be loved, and then he has become man to make it possible for us to love as he loved us.

—St. Mother Theresa[1]

WE WERE CREATED TO BE LOVED. Formed in the image and likeness of a God who is an eternal exchange of love, we were made to receive love and to give love. Quite simply, wounds form from either real or perceived failures to be loved the way we were created to be loved, or from being prevented from loving in the way that we were created to love.

What is love, though? When I speak of love, I'm not referring to a mere sentiment or feeling, but rather what the *Catechism* defines as "to will the good of another" (CCC 1766).

How can we love the way we were created to if we don't know what is good for another? We need to understand the

---

[1] St. Mother Teresa, "Mother Teresa Nobel Lecture," The Nobel Prize, December 11, 1979, https://www.nobelprize.org/prizes/peace/1979/teresa/lecture/.

goods that we were created to receive and that we should desire for one another.

The Six S's: The Goods We Were Created For

I have found that it can be helpful to think about the goods in a hierarchy, like a pyramid of goods. See, not all goods are equal. Some goods are lower or more basic, like goods concerning material possessions, and some goods are higher, such as goods related to the well-being of our soul. So the lowest levels of the pyramid comprise the most basic goods, with each subsequent level representing higher goods. This hierarchy of goods can be broken down into six S's: somatic, safety, sense of connection, self-esteem, self-excellence, and self-transcendence (see diagram below).

SELF-TRANSCENDENCE
Meaning, purpose, service, justice, beauty, truth, goodness, forgiveness, faith

SELF-EXCELLENCE
Desire to excel and be great in general and through particular tasks, competence, greatness, managing things well (time, money, etc.)

SELF-ESTEEM
Respect, status, recognition, esteem, dignity, value

SENSE OF CONNECTION
Friendship, family bonds, physical intimacy, sexual intimacy, connection with those we meet

SAFETY
Emotional, physical, interpersonal

SOMATIC
Physical needs, items related to the body, food, clothing, shelter, sleep, leisure, bodily health

Somatic Stuff. The most basic goods that we desire and for which we were created are *somatic goods*—the material and non-material things (like sleep!) related to the well-being of our bodies and ease in life. For example, we desire adequate shelter. We also want sufficient food to fuel our bodies and stock our cupboards. We desire clothing to wear; perhaps we desire a few pairs of shoes—a dress pair for work, a pair for exercise, and maybe a pair for daily activities. We also need sleep and exercise as well as items to help us engage in leisure, like books, music, maybe a fishing rod, and so forth. We likely desire some form of transportation to get us to work or school and a cell phone to contact friends and family. These are goods that relate directly to our bodily well-being.

Safety. Human beings want to feel a sense of safety. First, we desire physical safety. That is, we want to know that our physical bodies are not in threat or danger of being hurt, harmed, or violated in some way. We also desire financial safety; we want to have enough money to make ends meet and to buy the items that we need to survive and thrive. Along with financial safety, we also desire interpersonal safety, a sense of feeling as if our relationships are secure and that we have safe places for us to be ourselves—where we are known and can be vulnerable. Related to interpersonal safety is emotional safety. We desire to have our feelings acknowledged and respected. When I am sad or frustrated, I desire to have my feelings recognized by those to whom I show them. Now, this does not mean that one should indulge my feelings, but having our feelings acknowledged is a part of respecting the whole person.

Sense of Connection. The third level of goods relates to a sense of connection. We were made for connection and communion with others. It's natural to desire a sense of connection with family and friends. We desire close bonds and intimacy.

That is, we want people to see us for who we are and to desire to be close with us. We want to be known and to be trusted with knowing the vulnerable parts in others. Sense of connection includes not only emotional intimacy but also physical intimacy (including sexual intimacy) as well. Further, this sense of connection pertains to our relationship with God, the angels, and the saints.

Self-Esteem. We also have a desire for self-esteem. By self-esteem, I mean a sense of status and respect. We want to be recognized and valued. We are unique, unrepeatable, and irreplaceable creations of God. Our adoption as sons and daughters of our Heavenly Father endows us with great dignity. As such, a natural desire for respect, status, and recognition arises within us.

Self-Excellence. The next level of goods that we desire pertains to personal excellence. The tremendous physical feats accomplished by individual women and men throughout the ages speak to this desire in man. It is also evident in the unseen acts of heroism and virtue of the saints and holy women and men of God. Humans desire to push themselves to the limits to pursue excellence. We have a desire to want to excel and push ourselves to the extremes to seek what greatness lies within us. The great philosophers have recognized that the happy life is the life of virtue or excellence—embodying excellence in each of our powers and capacities. We want to excel and achieve competence and mastery in our lives.

Self-Transcendence. Deep within all of us lies a longing for that which is beyond us, greater than us. Self-transcendence comprises the most abstract goods that allow us to lose ourselves in something bigger than ourselves such as meaning,

A Bit about Wounds

purpose, beauty, truth, the pursuit of knowledge, goodness, justice, and making a gift of ourselves in service to others.

Each of these levels contains goods which we were created to possess and enjoy, goods that we desire. Everyone experiences a desire for the goods in this hierarchy. It is part-and-parcel of being human. In fact, an absence of desire for these things would be a problem in and of itself.

Wounds as an Absence of a Good, a Failure to Be Loved

Let's reiterate: we were created to receive and participate in the goods in the hierarchy—that is what love is, to be provided the goods for which we were created. Perfect love, God's love, provides the goods at each of these levels. Just look at the garden. Adam and Eve enjoyed God's perfect love and therefore lived without wounds before the Fall. God willed their good by providing to them the six S's. Adam and Eve wounded themselves, however, when they deprived themselves of communion with God, thereby disrupting the goods of sense of connection, interpersonal safety, and self-transcendence to name a few.

Each of our wounds can be traced back to the real or perceived thwarting of a good for which we were created. For example, I had a client who was incredibly competent in virtually every area of her life. She was in tremendous physical shape, running ultramarathons and engaging in a rigorous exercise routine. She was also an incredibly successful graduate student. Everything about this client screamed competent, respected, and valued. On the surface, she seemed to be flourishing, yet she was anxious and depressed.

In the course of therapy, she shared a pivotal memory. She remembered that as a little girl, her father would come home from work and kick back in his recliner. In all of her excitement and energy, she would run up to her father and start talking about her day and everything that happened. She said that she would never forget the look that her father gave—a look that said, "You're so annoying." This look communicated to her that she was a nuisance, that she wasn't respected or valued by her father, that he didn't want a relationship with her. Those looks left a deep wound in her. With those looks, her father unintentionally failed to show and provide her with the esteem, respect, and connection that she so desired. Turns out, much of the young woman's accomplishments were attempts to fill the gaping holes left by her father's looks.

Because we live in a fallen world, we constantly wound one another. As parents, siblings, friends, coworkers, and spouses, we're always falling short and failing to love those around us the way they deserve and desire to be loved; as a result, we create wounds in them and they create wounds in us.

Our Wounds Can Wreck Us

A wound causes suffering. Wounds are like holes—spaces where goods should be, but where we perceive an absence of the goods we desire and were created for. Wounds hurt. This is a fact that is undeniable and inescapable.

Being wounded is inevitable in this life, because the cross is inevitable in this life. Christ was wounded, and as His followers, we will be too. The suffering and hurt caused by our wounds are the cross in our lives. Yet, wounds heal over time if we pay attention to them, invite God into them, and *don't try to avoid* the suffering and hurt that accompanies them.

The crosses prepared for us by Christ, rather than the ones we've created for ourselves, have the power to sanctify, transform, and be a source of grace for us. The problem is, many of us aren't just carrying the cross Christ has made for us; we are

A Bit about Wounds

also carrying pain that we've caused ourselves by dealing with our suffering in unhealthy ways.

Primary and Secondary Wounds

So, it will be helpful to distinguish between two types of wounds—those we experience passively and those we contribute to. When we have been wounded in a completely passive way, that is, when we have not contributed to the wound, this is what we will call a *primary wound*. Primary wounds happen to us. Someone fails to love us in the way we were created to be loved, or we are denied the goods that we were created for. A clear example of a primary wound would be a parent who abandons or abuses their child. The parent's failure to value their child, to keep them emotionally and physically safe, and to establish loving social bonds are not the child's fault in any way. Primary wounds are synonymous with suffering. Suffering arises when we experience a primary wound.

Secondary wounds, on the other hand, are experiences of hurt due to our direct contribution. Secondary wounds are synonymous with pain. In secondary wounds, we manufacture pain by either 1) "priming the pump" or 2) enhancing and prolonging the suffering of a primary wound through false beliefs. When I say "priming the pump," I mean that through our beliefs, attitudes, behaviors, or habits we create an environment where there are increased odds or an increased likelihood of being wounded. Through excessive pursuit of the six S's or a desire to avoid emotional discomfort, we act out, we place ourselves in situations and engage in relationships that set us up to be hurt and wounded further. For example, imagine that I am a really angry father, always yelling, criticizing, and nitpicking at my kids. "Too much praise and a kid will get spoiled" is my motto. When I ask my kids to go fishing with me or to watch a show with me, they decline. They never want to talk about their day with me, only with their mother. I start to feel my desire to be an excellent and competent father dashed by my kids' actions. My bids for social connection with my kids are also thwarted by them.

Now, is the problem my kids? Not really. My anger, hypercriticism, and false beliefs create an environment in which my kids are likely not to want to be around me or share their daily experiences with me. I've created a situation which has a high probability of leaving me wounded. My wounds are secondary wounds because my kids aren't acting independently of me; they are *reacting* to me.

False Beliefs

Along with priming the pump, our false beliefs can cause secondary wounds by magnifying or extending the pain we feel. For example, let's say your father walked out on you when you were a young child. Since then, you've adopted the false belief that you need to have had a good father to be a good father. In such a case, you're setting yourself up, through your belief, for a secondary wound. See, a parent leaving hurts. It's a primary wound. Primary wounds cause suffering. However, my false belief that I need to have had a good dad to be a good dad deepens the suffering of the primary wound by ensuring that I will stay angry and resentful at my father on top of enduring the suffering of his absence. Further, on top of the resentment and anger I experience significant anxiety that I will harm a family of my own one day. My false belief causes me to experience added pain.

Take for example, a young woman who is sexually assaulted. Following the assault, she begins to believe that she is garbage, used goods, and that no man could love her. Not only will the young woman experience the suffering of being assaulted, of having her bodily security and autonomy

A Bit about Wounds

violated, but now her suffering is amplified by her subsequent false beliefs, as she imagines herself to be lonely and unlovable. Perhaps some of the most pernicious false beliefs, however, are those that begin with: "I'll be happy when_____." We fill in the blank with things like "I have enough money"; "my spouse stops being so distant"; "my kids start showing me respect"; "I get a promotion"; "my mom stops drinking"; "I lose twenty pounds"; "I get a girlfriend or boyfriend." The list goes on. By telling ourselves that our happiness is contingent or that it depends on others, we almost guarantee that we will experience secondary wounds. We're setting other people up to disappoint and hurt us, ensuring that we'll be anxious, angry, or unhappy. When people inevitably don't do what we want, we feel hurt and angered. Even if they do what we want or think we need to be happy, we feel anxious that they might stop and that it might all come to an end. Such false beliefs put people and situations in control of our happiness. We must begin to recognize how the false beliefs we bring to a situation contribute to our pain by either enhancing our existing pain or creating the opportunity to be hurt.

Avoidance: The Why of Secondary Wounds

Why do we contribute to further pain or secondary wounds? How does it all work? Oftentimes, after being wounded, we develop a false belief or series of false beliefs about the event or experience that caused the wound. For example, imagine someone who was bullied in school. Not only did they experience the suffering of not being respected, not having their dignity recognized, not being prized, but very often they adopt false beliefs that compound the primary wound: "I'm worthless"; "I'm garbage"; "No one likes me." These false beliefs are painful. A great truth about most humans is that we don't like discomfort and pain. Most of us want to avoid discomfort—painful memories, unpleasant thoughts, uncomfortable bodily experiences (e.g., racing heart, upset stomach, tightening chest, etc.). We want to push it away, distract ourselves from it, or convince ourselves it's not true.

Here's the kicker—*avoidance of suffering serves as the root cause of our additional pain*. In psychology this is called "experiential avoidance," and a significant amount of research has shown that this type of avoidance is related to emotional problems and psychological distress. Experiential avoidance "occurs when a person is unwilling to remain in contact with particular private experiences (e.g., bodily sensations, emotions, thoughts, memories, behavioral predispositions) and takes steps to alter the form or frequency of these events and the contexts that occasion them."[2] Many of us try to orchestrate our actions, relationships, and environments (our very lives) in ways that allow us to stay away from or reduce the suffering we experience from distressing emotions, memories, or feelings in our body. Yet, this traps us in a vicious cycle!

How? Well, we avoid the suffering through the extreme pursuit of the six S's. That is, we either overdevelop or underdevelop our pursuit of these goods in a bid to avoid suffering. Let's give an example. If we were bullied in school, then we might avoid the pain of feeling unlikable by either becoming invisible (extreme solitude), so no one will see us and we can't be hurt again, *or* by trying to make everyone like us and always being the center of attention (extreme esteem). Either way, we are trying to avoid the pain of feeling unlikable. Let's say we grew up in a home where there was significant financial instability. Some people cope with these negative memories and fears by becoming absolute pinchpennies,

---

[2] Steven C. Hayes, et al., "Experiential Avoidance and Behavioral Disorders: A Functional Dimensional Approach to Diagnosis and Treatment," *Journal of Consulting and Clinical Psychology* 64, no, 6 (1996): 1152–1154, 1168, https://doi.org/10.1037/0022-006X.64.6.1152.

A Bit about Wounds

caring only about saving money, while others avoid the suffering associated with these experiences by spending liberally and convincing themselves that they don't care about money at all. Or, if we feel an utter lack of control or autonomy in our marriage, we might pursue excessive control of our diet or in parenting.

As we pursue the extremes of the six S's, two things often happen. First, we become anxious, angry, and depressed because we are unable to completely avoid suffering. The world and the people in it just won't cooperate with our need to avoid suffering. Second, our world becomes small and narrow. We don't have access to the opportunities and experiences that lie outside of our purview, our overarching goal—and our goal has become avoiding suffering. Any relationship or activity that might activate suffering needs to be avoided.

So, we see that avoiding suffering has become a way of life for many of us. We've dealt with the suffering of primary wounds by employing various strategies to avoid the suffering. In doing so, we've set up circumstances and situations which are likely not only to allow us to be hurt again, but to leave us anxious, angry, unhappy, stressed, and the like.

Questions for Reflection

1. Can you identify ways that you engage in avoidance in your life? This could be avoidance of bad feelings, unpleasant thoughts, difficult situations, and the like.
2. What are the false beliefs that most commonly cause problems for you? Remember, you know that a belief is false because there is insufficient (or a total absence of) evidence to justify holding the belief. What things do you believe about yourself, your vocation, God, your value, other people, or the world that you do not have adequate evidence to justify believing? Sometimes our

beliefs are false because they are riddled with thought errors. See the list of common thought errors in Appendix D to see which ones you are prone to adopt.

Prayer

My Lord, help me to see all of the ways that I have contributed to my own pain. Show me the ways that I have contributed to my own suffering. Give me the courage and the wisdom to know when to approach, rather than avoid, difficult feelings, situations, and people. Replace the lies, falsehoods, and partial truths that I tell myself over and over with Your truth. Amen.

Chapter V

SELF-PRESERVATION: ACHIEVING SECURITY BY AVOIDING PAIN

The obstacle is in our "self," that is to say in the tenacious need to maintain our separate, external, egotistic will. . . . It is then the false self that is our god, and we love everything for the sake of this self.

—Thomas Merton[1]

UNTIL NOW, I'VE BEEN SPEAKING about avoiding pain, but another way of discussing the avoidance of pain is to speak of seeking security. All avoidance of pain is an attempt to experience security. So the beliefs, attitudes, and actions that contribute to our secondary wounds arise from our desire for security. They are self-preservation strategies, a term I will use throughout the rest of the book to encompass our attempts to seek security in order to avoid pain. We don't know how to manage our real or perceived feelings of vulnerability, so we turn to self-preservation. Whether someone is pinching

---

[1] Thomas Merton, *New Seeds of Contemplation* (Boston: Shambhala Publications, 2003), 23.

pennies or spending lavishly, both strategies are aimed at preserving their sense of security, preventing them from having to re-experience the pain of their past wounds.

A certain type of self-preservation is good; we should desire to keep ourselves safe from harm. We are not masochists. We should not go looking for pain and suffering. When we can reasonably avoid pain and suffering, we should! A woman in a physically abusive relationship should do everything in her power to avoid the abuser and to get away from the harmful situation. However, when we are not free to pursue God's voice and the action of the Holy Spirit in our lives, our self-preservation has gone too far. This type of self-preservation is harmful because it relies upon an extreme pursuit of some good to achieve our own preservation. We step outside of the reasonable or normal range of desiring the good and pursue it to the extreme—way too much or way too little.

Self-Preservation and Sin

This extreme pursuit of self-preservation can also be called sin. The *Catechism* tells us that sin is a "failure in genuine love for God and neighbor caused by a perverse attachment to certain goods" (CCC 1849) and that sin is "a revolt against God through the will to become 'like Gods,' knowing and determining good and evil" (CCC 1850). The self-preservation we're describing can rightly be called sin since a) we are failing by the pursuit of a good to the extreme and b) because we are relying upon ourselves and our own means to create a sense of security. This type of self-preservation comprises the various ways *we* attempt to control and manipulate the world and people around us to achieve a sense of security or avoid pain. These ways edge God out of the picture. They are *my* ways of dealing with *my* desires for good things in *my* time. In this

Self-Preservation: Achieving Security by Avoiding Pain

way, we choose our way, and do not allow God to be in control. We're pursuing our will, rather than the will of God. It's as if we say, "I'll take care of this one Lord. You don't know what I need. Doing your will won't provide me with the sense of security or avoidance of pain I want." I should note, however, that while the self-preservation I'm describing is sinful, it's likely that many individuals may not be culpable for these sins because these self-preservation strategies are often habitual, automatic, quasi-thoughtless behaviors.

Let's give an example. Imagine a young woman who grows up with an emotionally abusive mother. She also is never pursued by a young man in high school, making her feel ugly and undesirable. Though she believes she is called to marriage, she throws herself into her job and promoting various, important social justice causes, like the pro-life movement. By doing this, she avoids the pain of disappointment in not being asked out. She also avoids her fear of not being a good mother. So, she works hard, never putting herself in positions where she might meet a spouse. She never becomes emotionally involved or attached to any man. Ultimately, she is left with a general sense of "floating through life," a vague sense of depression, and a deep sense of loneliness. This young woman has decided to take her desire for security into her own hands. In this way, she sins; she cuts God out of the picture. She doesn't turn to Him for security, but rather handles life in her own way.

Habitual Sins and Our Wounds

It is not uncommon for our habitual sins, those frequent sinful behaviors that we confess (yelling at our children, impatience, lust, pornography, drug use and alcohol abuse, laziness, spiritual sloth, etc.) to be rooted in deep wounds. Let's use anger as an example. The anger that we experience with our children may just well be a self-preservation strategy to avoid some perceived suffering and to achieve one of the six S's. Anger and frustration toward your children might arise from being concerned with the esteem and respect of your friends (or your parents, in-laws, teachers at school). When your children act up or act out, you get worried and anxious that it will result in the loss of respect or esteem from others. Naturally, this makes you feel incredibly angry and anxious. If only your children would act the way that you need them to act, then you wouldn't have to feel worried about not being a good enough parent or not being respected by others. So, perhaps you become more authoritative, more punitive, yell louder, give bigger consequences. You would be happy if only they would behave. Or, maybe you avoid invitations to take your child places because it will activate your fear and anxiety.

Is the problem really your children's behavior, though? Not completely. The problem is the excessive desire to be esteemed and respected as a competent parent. Imagine if you weren't afraid of not being respected and weren't pursuing the esteem of others to the extreme. Then, while your children's behavior might be frustrating, it would not cause the excessive anger and anxiety that is currently your norm.

How about constantly being angry with your spouse? Perhaps you're consumed with a certain self-importance, guarding against the pain of a wound of feeling insignificant. In this self-importance, you feel like your day, your job, and your tasks are more important than that of your spouse. When you come home from work and your spouse doesn't ask about your day, you're left feeling resentful, angry, and hurt. Perhaps you even feel jealous and tell your spouse that they spend too much time talking to their friends and not enough time paying attention to you. Is the problem your spouse? Probably not. At least not completely. You'd experience significantly less hurt and pain if you weren't acting from a place of self-importance.

A Quick Word about Fear

I mentioned fear in the example above. Fear is a natural and good emotion. If you're looking down the snout of a bear, you should definitely feel fear. If a person is robbing you, you should feel fear! We experience fear when we anticipate the absence or diminishment of a good. Simply put, "F.E.A.R." is "Future Events Appearing Real." We feel fear when looking at the bear because we imagine the bear taking our life or severely maiming us; we imagine our family's pain in our absence. So, when I talk about fear as a character defect, I'm talking about an *excessive and self-centered worry* about the future loss of some good, not a proportionate and reasonable response to an event.

Fear is a pernicious and deceptive foe. For many of us, it penetrates virtually every aspect of our lives undetected. Excessive worry is one of the most pervasive bad habits of character, motivating many of our decisions and actions and causing many of our subsequent emotional disruptions. The difficulty with fear is that it can work on any level of the hierarchy of goods: fear about not having enough food, not being safe in our relationships, not having enough intimacy with our partner, not being respected at work, not thriving in our vocation, and not having a purpose. Imagining the absence or diminishment of one of the six S's, goods we were created for and desire, can cause tremendous fear. When we act out of fear, we seek to prevent some perceived future loss from occurring and in doing so we almost inevitably try to exercise excessive control over our circumstances and manipulate the people in our lives. Deep down, however, we intuitively know that we don't have the power to make life go our way. Our anxiety, depression, and frustration grow because the world and the people in it rarely stay in the place we put them! Ultimately, life happens as life does and we are left feeling burned, anxious, angry, and overwhelmed.

While we should pursue our good desires and preserve the goods we attain, problems with fear arise when we can't enjoy the present moment because we are so afraid about the potential future loss of good or the future failure to acquire a good that we think we need. Fear is excessive when it impedes our ability to freely love and follow God's daily call in our life. For example, heart disease runs rampant on both sides of my family. The thought of losing my life and my family if I were to die from a heart attack causes me fear. It should, to some extent. I should pursue bodily health and try to preserve the health I achieve. However, if I can't enjoy time with my family or life in general because my days are consumed with obsessing about healthy eating, reading labels, exercising, and worrying about what new fad I need to practice to avoid a heart attack, then my fear is too excessive. (As an aside, people will become annoyed with my health obsession and push back, avoid me, or tease me, leaving me feeling hurt.)

I'm reminded of the young man who was afraid of not being liked by his college peers because he had felt unloved and unwanted by his parents. He was so afraid that he would not connect with his friends that he constantly asked, "What can I do? Am I bothering you? Just let me know how I can be helpful." He asked so many times that his friends began to feel frustrated and distance themselves from him. Fear frequently causes the loss of the very thing that we are afraid of losing!

Back to the Problem

As we've noted, problems arise when we: a) adopt false beliefs or b) we adopt extreme self-preservation strategies in an

Self-Preservation: Achieving Security by Avoiding Pain

attempt to avoid pain. While these self-preservation strategies are meant to protect us, to keep us safe from perceived harm, ultimately, they create the very environments in which we are more likely to be harmed. We set the stage for secondary wounds through our false beliefs and self-protection behaviors and habits! We also set ourselves up to feel "stuck." As I see it, feeling stuck is often nothing more than our old self-preservation strategies no longer working in our current situation.

Let's give one more example to put all of the pieces together. Imagine a young man who grew up in poverty due to his parents' drug addiction. The young man never knows when he will eat a meal and only has a few pairs of clothes (i.e., absence of somatic goods like food and clothing) because his parents squander food and clothing money on drugs (absence of security, i.e., financial). The young man is teased at school because of his dirty clothes (absence of self-esteem, i.e., respect). Eventually, the young man's father overdoses and dies, and his mother's addiction causes her to leave him to be raised by his grandmother (absence of social connection, i.e., love of parents). He develops false beliefs: "I'm not lovable"; "If I don't care for myself no one will"; "People always leave"; "I can't be a good parent because I haven't had good parents." The false beliefs that accompany the primary wounds add more pain to the already painful primary wounds; the false beliefs are in themselves a secondary wound. He now has the primary pain of having parents leave, lacking sufficient material support, and being disrespected in school, as well as the secondary pain of imagining that he is unlovable and is destined to be a bad parent and of feeling afraid that he won't have his material needs met.

To avoid this pain, the young man engages in an *excessive* attempt to have his desire for the material and financial goods met; his fear is an excessive concern that he will lose or fail to attain sufficient material goods and financial security. He's seeking security; he's protecting himself and greed is the means. His greed is really just a self-preservation strategy. With his greed and fear, however, come other problems. Interpersonal relationships are harmed because the young man is more concerned with achieving a sense of financial and material security than attending to others' needs in relationships; people become instruments to be used to achieve financial security and to avoid suffering. The young man feels like other people don't want to be around him (secondary wound). But hasn't he been the catalyst for this because of how he's chosen to deal with the pain of his wound? The man ends up working seventy-five to ninety hours a week providing a financially secure living for his family but has strained, unstable, loveless relationships with his children. He feels angry at his kids for not properly appreciating his hard work. Yet hasn't he set himself up to feel frustrated because he's only working to prove to himself and others that he's valuable and lovable? Further, other people in the young man's life feel resentful at how he hoards material goods and has to be the center of attention, which causes resentment, tension, and envy—secondary wounds that cause the man suffering.

We can see from this example that for some of us, our chronic anger, stress, anxiety, depression, social phobia, and unhappiness are rooted in our false beliefs and our extreme self-preservation strategies. Often these self-preservation strategies become deeply ingrained in our personalities; they become habitual. As we continually use these strategies to try and achieve a sense of security, avoiding the pain of our wounds, we only create circumstances and situations which make us more likely to be wounded. Eventually, our self-preservation becomes our own prison! Our world gets smaller and smaller as we strive to control our pain.

To begin the healing process, we must identify our

Self-Preservation: Achieving Security by Avoiding Pain

false beliefs and our extreme self-preservation habits. We'll borrow from Alcoholics Anonymous and call these excessive strategies for avoiding pain *defects of character* or *character shortcomings*. It is these defects of character that cause a significant portion of our problems. Below is a list of the common defects of character. Take a look at them and familiarize yourself with them, because it's important to know the culprits responsible for our pain.

Resentments	Jealousy
Worry	Envy
Self-justification	Laziness
Self-importance	Procrastination
Self-condemnation	Insincerity
Self-pity	Excessively negative thinking
Lying	Lust
Impatience	Perfectionism
Hate	Criticism, gossip
False pride	Greed

Questions for Reflection

1. What are the habitual sins that you find yourself confessing repeatedly? Can you see how they may be rooted in self-preservation?

2. When you think about letting go of your self-preservation strategies, what thoughts or feelings arise for you?

3. Which defects of character do you most identify with? Do any immediately stand out to you as ones you might possess?

Prayer

Come Holy Spirit! Spirit of power and healing. Spirit of peace and protection. Help me to know that You are my protector. In Your will, I will find the security that I seek. Help me to see the ways that I rely upon my own ideas and methods, rather than on You. If You are for me, who can stand against me? Allow those words to take root deep within me: Even in the darkest and hardest moments, You are for me, Holy Spirit. You will provide for me because I am one of the Father's beloved. Amen.

Chapter VI

TYPES OF HEALING & HEALING THE CONSCIENCE

For in my wounded heart, I have seen the shining of Thy splendor.
—*St. Augustine*[1]

REMEMBER, TO BE HEALED is to be made free—free to love and serve God and our fellow man. Healing allows us to pursue God's call in our lives; that is, to have the interior freedom to be able to go where the Lord calls us and do what He asks of us. When we are unhealed, we are bound by our feelings, our memories, and our negative thought patterns, and we are prevented or obstructed from pursuing love and God's voice in our life.

Two Types of Healing

In considering what this freedom looks like, it is helpful to discuss two different types of healing. First, there is a healing

---

[1] Augustine, *Confessions*, ed. Michael P. Foley, trans. F. J. Sheed (Indianapolis, IN: Hackett, 2007), 10.41, pp. 254–55.

that's brought about by the removal of a defect—the unpleasant emotions, defects of character, or the patterns of thought that give rise to emotional suffering are simply removed by the Lord. They are gone. There's a second type of healing, however, that we'll call redemptive healing. In this case, God doesn't remove the problem, but buys it back for Himself to use as He wills!

Removal Healing. Let's discuss removal healing first. It is the case sometimes that when we bring a certain defect, negative thought pattern, unhelpful belief, particular fear, or bad habit to the Lord, He removes this issue completely from our life. This type of healing can feel dramatic.

I think for many of us, when we think of healing, this is the type of healing that we envision. It's something akin to the healing of a physical wound; where there was once an open wound, there is now only healed skin. And while physical wounds sometimes leave scars, in some instances, the skin grows back in such a way that one would never even know that there had been a wound. Something similar can and does happen with our emotional wounds.

Many of the physical healings in the Gospels seem to be total removal, healings in which the root problem is completely taken away. Take the blind man, for example. Jesus mixes spit with mud, rubbing it on the eyes of the blind man. The man's eyesight is completely restored. There are no remaining effects of blindness (to the best of our knowledge). Where there was once a defect, there is now perfect vision. Or, returning to the example of the paralytic man lowered through the roof by his friends: he, too, was healed completely by our Lord. Our Lord's words remove the man's inability to walk. His physical health is fully restored. These physical healings show us the freedom that the Lord gives to those whom He heals in the Gospel. They receive a freedom from the suffering and the hurt associated with their physical ailment. They receive a freedom from the deficit and defect in their bodies. Not only is this type of healing possible in the body, but it's possible in our emotions and psychological constitution as well. It is something that the Lord does in the lives of many and may do for you as you implement the steps I lay out in this book. It may happen slowly over time or it may happen in an instant, but it can and does happen.

However, you might not experience the removal of your psychological struggles at all.

Redemptive Healing. There's another legitimate and important type of healing. This is a healing that does not remove the suffering associated with one's wound, yet still sets the person free. I call this healing redemptive healing. The name refers to the idea that God uses our very wound in His service, making it a source of healing for others. The model for this type of healing is St. Paul. We read in Paul's second letter to the Corinthians:

> And to keep me from being too elated by the abundance of revelations, a thorn was given me in the flesh, a messenger of Satan, to harass me, to keep me from being too elated. Three times I begged the Lord about this, that it should leave me; but he said to me, "My grace is sufficient for you, for my power is made perfect in weakness." (2 Cor 12:7–9)

St. Paul is given a thorn in his flesh. While there is debate among theologians what the thorn in his flesh represents, there is no doubt that, based on its description, it caused suffering. It was a problem for St. Paul. He had a wound.

How does St. Paul deal with this suffering in his life? With this wound? Well, naturally, he asked the Lord to remove it. Three times, in fact! Despite St. Paul's pleading, the Lord does not remove the thorn in his flesh. Now, this is St. Paul we're talking about. St. Paul, who had seen the risen Christ, a holy and zealous man! Yet, the Lord doesn't remove this thorn. Why not?

We certainly don't want to say that the Lord did not heal St. Paul or that the Lord left St. Paul a slave to his pain and his wounds. The Lord tells Paul that His grace is sufficient. No, in fact, what the Lord's grace ensures is that St. Paul can follow His voice and His will wherever he is called and bring the thorn with him. His wound isn't removed, but Paul doesn't need to have the thorn removed in order to experience freedom. Rather, Paul is given the freedom to pursue and do the Lord's bidding, despite the wound.

Most of us spend our lives trying to control our environments and orchestrate our surroundings so that our wounds, our thorns are not touched—so that we don't suffer. A wound, just like a thorn, causes suffering when touched. So, most of us walk through life, trying to sidestep anything that might aggravate our suffering (remember experiential avoidance?). We may feel like the Lord is calling us in a particular direction, to a particular job, or to a specific relationship, but we quickly realize that we can't go in that direction because to do so would mean that our thorn is possibly aggravated. Or, if we do go where the Lord is calling us, we engage in self-preservation strategies, which prevent us from being free, effective instruments of God's grace. Perhaps we take the job God has called us to, but we procrastinate, overachieve, act out of chronic anger or greed, and so forth. In this way, we are in bondage to our wounds, and our capacity to act in love and service to God and to our fellow man is greatly diminished. So, we either avoid going in a particular direction or we have to control the path in such a way that we aren't hurt. We are slaves to our pain.

St. Paul is given tremendous grace not to be a slave to his pain. He's not worried about avoiding negative or uncomfortable experiences caused by having his thorn touched. He's given the freedom to pursue the call of the Lord. This is where life begins to take on a new sense of purpose and meaning. Our purpose and meaning in life depend upon being able to follow the Lord's call each day. The Lord calls us to a mission, to a purpose. If we spend our life avoiding pain, we can't follow our mission or purpose with the complete freedom it demands.

Healing Our Conscience

Very often in our attempts to protect and defend ourselves, we hurt and wound others through our defects of character. Sometimes these harms are large and obvious, and sometimes they are small and go unnoticed by us. They do not, however, go unnoticed by our conscience.

By acting in ways that hurt others, we also hurt ourselves—we violate our conscience. What is our conscience, though? Our conscience is God's commands written deep within our own hearts. The *Catechism* articulates the definition of conscience well:

> Conscience is a judgment of reason whereby the human person recognizes the moral quality of a concrete act that he is going to perform, is in the process of performing, or has already completed. In all he says and does, man is obliged to follow faithfully what he knows to be just and right. It is by the judgment of his conscience that man perceives and recognizes the prescriptions of the divine law. (CCC 1778)

Our conscience is that place within us that judges whether an action we've done, are doing, or are going to do is good and morally right. Conscience is able to judge these actions because it contains within it a fundamental law written by God: do what is good and avoid evil. Now, we must take this fundamental law and form it, growing in our understanding of what is good and the conditions and factors that relate to evil. This fundamental law must be educated over the course of our lives. Nevertheless, this inscription on our heart by God to do good and avoid evil allows us to make judgments about actions, which we must obey.

What should we do when we've behaved in a way that violates our conscience and contradicts the law written on our heart? The healthy way to remedy this violation is through the process of *remorse, confession, atonement, reconciliation,* and *justification.*

The work by the political philosopher, Dr. J. Budziszewski (pronounced bud-es-chef-ski), on conscience is really wonderful and helpful here. If we violate our conscience and we don't pay, or assuage our conscience in the proper way, our conscience tries to assuage itself in the closest way possible through what Budziszewski calls the "five Furies." The Furies are the unhealthy ways that our conscience seeks to assuage itself when it has been violated. The Furies are like the shadow side of the healthy process to assuage conscience.

Remorse

The first of the Furies is related to remorse. In its healthy expression, one should experience a feeling of remorse after doing something wrong and flee from the wrong that they've done. However, in its unhealthy expression, rather than fleeing the wrong and experiencing remorse, one simply avoids thinking about the wrong they've done. They flee from thinking about the hurtful event.

For some of us, if we have done a wrong or evil to another, we avoid thinking about the evil or wrong by turning to alcohol or drugs to dull our memory of the event. We may also distract ourselves with social media, binge watch TV, avoid situations that might remind us of the wrong, or simply stay super busy. We flee from thinking about the wrong we've done by changing the language we use to discuss it, pretending that the evil we've done is something else. For example, rather than admitting that we are excessively beating our children, we say that we are "disciplining them" in order to avoid thinking about what we are really doing.

Confession

The second of the Furies is related to confession. In its healthy expression, one confesses the wrong that they have done. When we fail to pay conscience this due, however, the price is constantly sharing all the details of our life, except the one thing that matters—the confession of the deed we've done along *with the admission that it was wrong.*

We're familiar with the people who overshare the most morally bankrupt and evil deeds of their lives in order to "get it off their chest." This is often a sign of shame, an indication that the person has yet to confess that the deed itself was wrong. Conscience is not satisfied, so they tell the story over and over to whoever will listen. They are confessing the incorrect aspect of the experience. They openly confess the details, but hide the admission that the act itself was wrong.

Atonement

The third Fury is related to atonement. In its healthy expression, when we harm someone, we repay the debt that is owed them. If we steal money, we pay it back; if we crash a car, we pay for the damage. The Fury of atonement occurs when we fail to pay a debt that we know is owed due to our actions.

Budziszewski likens it to trying to pay off a loan shark; you constantly pay interest, but you never pay off the principle.

For some, this may take the form of actually embracing the suffering related to their harmful or evil deed, because they feel as if it's the price they should pay. It's as if the suffering makes the deed acceptable. False atonement doesn't pay back the debt that's owed, even if it reduces our remorse. Inevitably, the need to atone returns. I'm reminded here of a Vietnam veteran I had worked with. A young child had killed some members of his squad. As the young boy was slowly reloading his weapon, a gun that was too big for him, the veteran shot and killed him. The veteran told me that he was fairly certain he could have run to the child and stopped him from reloading, but that he shot and killed him in his anger. Guess what career that veteran went on to pursue after the war? He became a second-grade schoolteacher.

Reconciliation

The fourth Fury is related to reconciliation. When we act in an evil or harmful way, we frequently sever our bonds of communion and union with others, including God. So, in its healthy expression, reconciliation seeks to reestablish the social bonds that have been damaged or destroyed by our actions. In its unhealthy expression, reconciliation drives us toward establishing bonds with people who have done similar wrongs—thieves hang with thieves.

The expression "water seeks its own level" fits this fourth Fury. Our need for social connection is so innate that when we sever bonds with people because of our actions, if we don't reconcile with them, we tend to hang out with people who have done the harms and evils we've done. Shared guilt unites people! Another unhealthy expression of reconciliation is forming very strong bonds with the person we are harming. I'm reminded of a young woman who was using serious street drugs with her boyfriend. In their active addiction, while they were high, they would physically and emotionally abuse one another. Rather than being driven apart, they would feel closer after these outbursts, as if they were the only two that could really understand each other. Further, they each began to believe, "Well I must really be in love if I let the person treat me like that." Each feels guilty for hurting the other and for allowing themselves to be treated so poorly. Guilt binds.

Justification

The fifth and final Fury is related to justification. In its healthy expression, justification means getting back into the right, or being brought into harmony with justice. In its unhealthy form, justification expresses itself in self-justification, rationalization, and excuses.

We are often masters at making excuses or justifying why what we did wasn't really wrong. In this way, rather than aligning ourselves with justice, we try to align justice with ourselves. That is, we don't conform to what is right; we try to conform what is right to our actions. I'm reminded of an incident with two of my sons. The older child was frustrated with the younger child for looking over his shoulder while he watched a video on the iPad. He reacted strongly and said some mean things to his younger brother. When my wife and I pulled him aside to talk to him about the incident, he gave us a barrage of excuses, all justifying to us why his actions weren't really that bad. The more we pushed back, the more he made excuses. His conscience was raging! His emotion, frustration, and anger grew. All he needed to do was say, "I messed up. I shouldn't have talked to him like that," hugged his brother, and tried to talk nicely to him and he would have felt better. Since he wouldn't, he fell prey to the Furies.

Why do these Furies matter? Well, we need to recognize where we have harmed others because some of the discomfort, stress, and dysfunction we may be experiencing in our lives could be due to the Furies. The Furies can serve as blocks to God's grace in our lives. They are unhealthy ways that our conscience tries to assuage itself. In this way, the Furies prevent us from living freely, since they compel us to seek counterfeit satisfaction for our conscience. Therefore, if we are going to heal, we must identify the wrongs we have done to others in our lives and go through a healthy process of remorse, confession, atonement, reconciliation, and justification.

Putting It All Together

Let's summarize. If we can identify the bad character habits in our lives, then we can see the problems they are causing. The defects of character block us from the light of God's love and grace. They are an armor, which we believe keeps us safe, but which blocks us from the action of His grace and the sound of His voice. Sometimes God will completely remove these barriers if we ask Him. Other times, like for St. Paul, our wounds will remain, but they will now become instruments of the Lord. He will use our wounds to bring about healing, compassion, and mercy in the lives of others, and in doing so give our own suffering a tremendous sense of purpose and meaning.

When we act out of our self-preservation strategies, we are usually increasing the chances that we will hurt or harm others. In such cases, we must recognize these harms, no matter how small, because our conscience is seeking satisfaction for having violated it. If we desire emotional healing, then we must root out our bad character habits and make right the wrongs of our past!

Types of Healing & Healing the Conscience

Questions for Reflection

1. How have you dealt with wrongs that you've done to others in the past?
2. Do any of the Furies stand out to you as relevant or present in your life? Can you tie this Fury to a particular way you've betrayed your conscience?

Prayer

Oh Blessed Trinity, help me to hear Your voice deep within my conscience. Place in me the desire for freedom—a desire to love as You call me to love. Help me to see the ways I fail to love like You, to love the way I am called to love, and grant me the grace of repentance. Let me turn back to You with all my heart, willing to right any wrongs that I have done to others. Amen.

Chapter VII
STEPS ONE AND TWO

IF YOU'VE MADE IT THIS FAR, hopefully you're now convinced that 1) we all suffer, 2) the path to healing begins with the complete surrendering of our attitudes, ideas, and behaviors, and 3) God wants to heal us. Further, you should have a better understanding of how and why our wounds form and how we heal.

So far, what we've discussed in previous chapters is all theoretical, but it's not enough to just think about healing. Healing requires action. So, in this chapter, I'd like to lay out the first two of six steps that will walk us through the actual process of healing. These steps are intended to be sequential, in that they will build upon insights from the previous steps, so it's important to work each step fully and to the best of your ability before moving on to the next step.

STEP ONE: *Humbly acknowledge that I am struggling and that left to my own devices, my life is not fulfilling.*

Scripture for Meditation: "I am the vine, you are the branches. He who abides in me, and I in him, he it is that bears much fruit, for apart from me you can do nothing" (John 15:5).

Virtue: Humility

We can't heal if we don't admit that there is something in need of healing. Further, we won't turn to God as long as we rely upon ourselves. So, the first step is admitting that there are problems in our life that we can't adequately handle. Oftentimes, admitting that we have problems can be incredibly difficult. We spend such a significant amount of time and energy trying to build up an image of ourselves as healthy and successful, trying to "stay positive." It can be humbling and scary, and we can even erroneously feel like a failure if we admit that we have issues—to admit that there are areas in our life that we do not know how to adequately deal with, to admit that we need help.

Apart from Christ we can do nothing! We have to admit our lack of power if we are going to open ourselves up to His power! For too long we have been relying upon ourselves in sneaky, subtle, and even unrealized ways. We have been relying upon our own strength, abilities, and ideas to get what we want, what we think we need, and to achieve a sense of security.

That is why the virtue associated with the first step is humility. This kind of admission of powerlessness requires an honest capacity to look at oneself and to recognize in truth one's genuine deficiencies and strengths. Openly admitting to and exposing the areas of our life where we are hurting, broken, or feel insecure can feel very scary and vulnerable. Humility allows us to look at ourselves as we truly are and to acknowledge our limits and our shortcomings. Cultivating humility in the first step is crucial for all of the other

Steps One and Two

steps because, as St. Thomas suggests, humility is foundational to spiritual growth in the sense that it removes the obstacle of pride "which 'God resisteth,' and makes man submissive and ever open to receive the influx of Divine grace. Hence it is written (James 4:6): 'God resisteth the proud, and giveth grace to the humble.'"[1] If the virtues of the other steps are to take hold in more than mere appearance, then we must grow in genuine humility.

In truthfully acknowledging the areas in which we are struggling, we carve out space, which we had previously tried to fill with the image, appearance, and efforts of "being okay." By carving out this space, we begin to create a vacuum, or something of a spiritual black hole, that attracts God's grace. The humble soul is fertile soul for grace because it readily recognizes where it is in need. The humble heart does not pretend; it does not wear a mask or a facade; it is genuine and authentic. It is not constantly busy and moving with effort, but still and peaceful in its circumstances.

He is the vine and we are the branches. So, in this first step, we are asked humbly to acknowledge who we truly are—not who we want the world to see us as, or how we want to be perceived, but to admit to the areas in our life where we are struggling, stumbling, or failing. Maybe it's our finances, our relationship with one of our children, our sexuality, or our career. This first step invites us not only to recognize the areas that need healing, but also to acknowledge that we are incapable of fixing them in and of ourselves. We lack the sufficient power.

What are the concrete actions associated with the first step? We can begin by praying every day for the virtue of

---

[1] Thomas Aquinas, *Summa Theologica*, 2nd and rev. ed., trans. Fathers of the English Dominican Province (London: Burns, Oates & Washburn, 1920; New Advent, 2017): I-II, q. 161, a. 4, ad 2, https://www.newadvent.org/summa/3161.htm; emphasis added.

humility. A good place to start is with the Litany of Humility. Upon waking in the morning, pray this Litany. If there is another prayer that you prefer or if you'd rather simply ask for humility in a prayer from the heart, then do it. The important thing is to beg for the increase in this virtue and to make yourself aware of your need for it. End your day with a prayer for humility as well. Don't just think about praying; actually ask God for humility. And don't just pray once. Pray for humility daily, in the morning and in the evening.

Next, spend some time meditating on the Scripture verse of the vine and branches (John 15:5). When you're finished, make a list of any relationship, situation, organization, or area of your life where you are struggling; feeling unhappy, unfulfilled; experiencing anxiety, stress, or chronic anger. Perhaps there are people you've struggled to forgive. Maybe you've avoided thinking about a person(s) who you have harmed. Where are the areas of unspoken, unacknowledged suffering, hurt, and pain in your life? Are there any personality traits, characteristics, or behaviors that in truth, in humility, you are now willing to admit are problematic or causing difficulty? What attitudes, ideas, and behaviors are you now willing to put under the purifying light of God's love?

STEP TWO: Examine our understanding of God, and where it is distorted. Pray for it to be corrected.

Scripture for Meditation: "For I know the plans I have for you, says the LORD, plans for welfare and not for evil, to give you a future and a hope" (Jer 29:11).

Virtue: Faith

To bring resolution and peace to our lives, we need God's power. Step two requires that we recognize that we may have distorted and inaccurate views of God. We do not experience God as loving. Yet, Jesus wants to reconcile our hearts and minds to His, to the very life of the Blessed Trinity, and in doing so, to heal us. Many of us have a hard time believing that God wants to heal us, that God loves us unconditionally. Our distorted and false beliefs about God's character impede us from genuinely approaching Him and cause us to keep an emotional distance from Our Lord.

God Attachment

In psychology, there is a distinction between what we know about God (sometimes called "God concept" or "God image") and how we feel about God—our attachment to God. "God image" is the cognitive view of God that we have. It's the idea of God that we've learned in Catechism classes. Most of us know the right answer when it comes to who God is; we know it in our head, but we don't feel it in our heart—God is love, mercy, protector, Father, and so on.

"God attachment," on the other hand, like caregiver-child attachment, is the felt experience of security that we have with God. While most Catholics have a very positive God image, their God attachment is oftentimes less secure than they realize or would like to admit.

Research shows that our pattern or template for how we emotionally relate to God comes from our relationship with our caregivers. That is, we use our experience with early childhood caregivers as the lens and pattern through which we see and experience our relationship with God. It is not a genuine and authentic relationship with us as we are, or with God as He is. So, if we had an insecure attachment to our parents, we're likely to have an insecure attachment to God, avoiding emotional intimacy with Him. If on the other hand, we had a secure attachment to our parents, that is, we experienced felt security with them, viewed them as a safe haven, and experienced them as a safe base for exploration, then we will likely view God in a similar way.

If we have an insecure attachment to God, then we will naturally struggle to believe that God wants to heal us. We will be distrustful of His love for us. We won't feel safe and secure. We need to take time to consider how we really feel about God. Do we feel safe and secure? Do we *feel* like He's a loving, tender father? Or are we distrustful or disinterested or apathetic toward God?

The virtue of faith is associated with this step. The *Catechism* tells us, "Faith is the theological virtue by which we believe in God and believe all that he has said and revealed to us, and that Holy Church proposes for our belief, because he is truth itself" (CCC 1814). We must begin to believe in God as He is and as He has revealed Himself, not as an extension of our parents. St. John tells us that "God is love" (1 John 4:8).

What are the concrete actions of the second step? First, we begin by praying for the theological virtue of faith. We pray that we might come to know God as He has revealed Himself. We ask God that we might know His very heart! Next, we evaluate our relationship with our parents. We should write down on paper the answers to the following questions: To what extent did we feel safe with them? To what extent do we feel seen by them? Did we feel deeply understood? Sometimes in the attachment literature, researchers will talk about this as "feeling felt." Did we feel felt by our parents? Did they respond in warm and compassionate ways? Were they cold, harsh, distant, or dismissive? Could we count on their love consistently? Were they inconsistent?

Now it will help us to turn to our relationship with God. How do we respond to God? Do we turn to Him and show Him the depths of our hearts and our fears? If not, why not? What are we afraid of? How do you think He might respond? Why would He respond this way? Write down and explore the ways in which your relationship with God mirrors your relationship with your caregivers. You may uncover some significant similarities. But that is not enough. In this step we must begin anew to encounter God with trust. We must try to rebuild this relationship with God from the ground up because we will not have the courage or the interest in presenting our deep wounds to a God who we are afraid of, anxious about, or think might be disinterested in us. It will help us to start by making a list of all of the characteristics that you want God to possess. What are the traits that you desire in God? Now write a list of what you need from God. Do you need Him to just listen? Do you need God be the one person in your life who doesn't need you to perform? Lastly, you should write down the words that you want or need to hear God say to you. What do you need Him to speak to your heart? Write these words or phrases down and take them to prayer.

Moving forward, we should try to pray to God, focusing on the characteristics that we most want Him to possess. As you pray, imagine those characteristics that you deeply want and desire God to possess, and bring them to your imagination as you are praying to God. Take time and bring to your mind how the most loving, caring person you know would respond to you. What would their tone of voice sound like? Would they gently and compassionately touch you? Would they hug you? What would they say? Imagine God responding to you in this way, in tone and touch, as you pray—whenever you bring yourself into His presence. Using your imagination in this way will allow you to re-envision, over time, a God who is trustworthy and loving. Also, allow God to speak the words that you need or want to hear from Him.

Further Action Steps

1. Read the Surrender Novena (appendix A). What words or phrases resonate with you? Which words or phrases trouble you? Why? Repeat the words of surrender throughout the day, allowing them to penetrate deep into your heart.

2. Pray the Litany of Trust (appendix A) each day along with the Surrender Novena. Imagine the characteristics (e.g., gentleness, mercy, power, etc.) Our Lord must have in order for you to say, "Jesus, I trust in You." As you pray the Litany, imagine Our Lord possessing those characteristics.

Chapter VIII

STEPS THREE AND FOUR

STEP THREE: Identify your character defects, the causes and conditions of your unhappiness.

Scripture for Meditation: "Why do you see the speck that is in your brother's eye, but do not notice the log that is in your own eye? Or how can you say to your brother, 'Let me take the speck out of your eye,' when there is the log in your own eye? You hypocrite, first take the log out of your own eye, and then you will see clearly to take the speck out of your brother's eye" (Matt 7:3–5).

Virtue: Courage

In steps one and two, we built the necessary foundation to engage in step three. We've admitted that there are areas of our lives in which we are struggling, that we are having problems that we can't sufficiently deal with on own power. We've begun to remove the mask of self-sufficiency, the mask of the false self, but it's not enough. We must identify the specific situations, people, organizations, and most importantly, the exact defects of character that are causing us problems.

This takes tremendous courage. To identify those parts of ourselves that we've spent so much time concealing, indulging, or ignoring is no small task. We may discover aspects of ourselves that we once thought were assets, but now recognize as defects. We will finally take stock of what's truly within us. Most people experience tremendous fear at this prospect. Many of us would rather fight in real battles than approach the dragons within! This is why the virtue for the third step is courage.

My Wounds

What are the concrete actions associated with the third step? We should begin this step and each subsequent time we sit down to work on this step with a prayer for honesty and courage. Next, we should begin with a piece of paper and divide that paper into four columns. In the first column you should write down all of the people you can remember who've wounded you (where the wounds still trouble you). Where should you start? At the very beginning. We must be thorough and leave nothing out, at least not intentionally. So, starting with your earliest memories, work your way chronologically through your life. Identify all of the people, organizations, or institutions that hurt you. How do you know if the wound still troubles you? Well, one way to determine this is to imagine bumping into the person on the street or at the mall or stepping back into the organization or institution. Do you re-experience some of the same feelings that you felt when they hurt you? Do you feel shame, embarrassment, anger, anxiety, stress, sadness, and the like? If you feel anger or re-experience some of the same feelings you did in the original experience, then the wound likely still bothers you. In that case, write it down. No wound is too small. We may tell ourselves that we shouldn't still feel hurt or the incident was really small, so it shouldn't bother us. Ignore this voice. Leave nothing out. Get it all on paper.

Next, in the second column, write down what the person or organization did to hurt you. This does not need to be a long, detailed story, just bullet points that will help you remember the events or actions that contributed to the wound. You will share the details of the story later. You just need to write something to jog your memory in the second column. Write down all of the harms done to you by the person or organization.

Now, the third column helps us understand why this action or behavior hurt us. In the third column you'll look at the six S's in the hierarchy of goods and determine which good you experienced an actual or perceived deprivation of. Be specific. Which good was not received, was thwarted, denied, or diminished to cause the wound?

My Part: Self-Preservation, Dishonesty, Fear

The fourth column represents a shift of sorts. In this column, we're not concerned with what has been done to us, but instead we are now interested in how we've contributed to the wound. We want to look for our part. Where have we have either set the conditions—primed the pump—to be wounded, or, where have we magnified or extended our pain through false beliefs and fears? In particular, we want to look for *self-preservation*, *dishonesty*, and *fear*. Of all of the columns, this one is the most important because it represents the column that you actually have some control over. If we can begin to see our part in our hurts, pains, and unhappiness, then we can begin to change.

So, in this fourth column we want to first identify the

self-preservation strategies that we brought into a situation that may have contributed to our wound. Imagine the young man who always feels like he needs to talk or dominate conversations for fear that someone might ask him a question that might make him feel stupid. His constant talking becomes annoying and frustrating to his peers. They no longer want to spend time with him. The young man has created his own pain by contributing to the situation that has left him feeling hurt (i.e., not being invited to hang out with his peers). This column should identify those self-preservation strategies that set the stage for us to be hurt or which directly lead to us being hurt (e.g., acting out of anger to dominate someone and them reacting in a way that hurts us). Through our self-preservation strategies, we pursue what we want, and when the world or those in it don't act in accord with what we want, we feel threatened—they are jeopardizing our security—which causes pain.

We must also identify our dishonesty in this column. Dishonesty includes actually lying to others, and also the lies we tell ourselves. Our false beliefs are in fact lies that we tell ourselves. False beliefs are beliefs that lack sufficient evidence or are contradicted by evidence. It will help us to see the often unrecognized ways we lie to ourselves through false beliefs which exacerbate, enlarge, or extend our pain. If my wound is a primary wound, I can enlarge or extend it by telling myself things like "I'll never be the same"; "I'll never get over this"; "I won't be able to be happy until this ends." What are the false beliefs we brought into the situation that contribute to the pain we're experiencing? What are our false beliefs about ourselves, others, and the world? Was I placing an unrealistic expectation on someone (e.g., my spouse should always be available to talk)? Did we hang our happiness on someone or something (e.g., I'll be happy when . . . I get that promotion)?

Finally, the fourth column should identify our fears and

the role they play in creating misery for us. When I possess a deeply held fear going into a situation, or act out of fear in a situation, I'm resting my well-being on life's events and on others' actions. That is, if people don't act in certain ways or life doesn't go the way I desire, then it confirms or triggers my fear and causes me pain and distress. Activated fear results in—you guessed it—self-preservation strategies. A vicious cycle.

You should probably have a few pages of writing at this point. Getting the fourth column right is important because it represents the things we can change. Many of us have spent long amounts of time, effort, and energy trying to control life and those around us. What we will find is that life begins to improve to the extent that we can identify and begin to rid of ourselves of our various self-preservation strategies, dishonesties, and fears—the ways we contribute to our own misery. Life will have certain sufferings, but we will not be adding to them any longer. If we can begin to identify how we add to life's sufferings, we will be well on our way to accepting life as life is.

Benefits: Forgiveness and Reality Check

There are two benefits from recognizing the part we play in our pain. First, as we learn to identify and acknowledge our self-preservation strategies—that is, the ways we are cut off from God—we realize that many of the behaviors in others that we dislike or that have hurt us are actually their own self-preservation strategies. Just like being cut off from God resulted in us hurting others, so too do the security-seeking strategies of others hurt us. Seeing the depths of our own character defects helps us grow in compassion and understanding for others. We are more likely to be forgiving as we see ourselves in others. Second, by identifying our part in our pain, we begin to see just how self-focused we really are. Though we've considered ourselves thoughtful and considerate, we now begin to see just how many ways we are actually self-centered rather than God-centered. Even when we thought that we were acting to help others, we now recognize a dual motivation employed to help us avoid pain, or to manipulate circumstances to our emotional benefit. We can now see on paper just how cut off from the Holy Spirit we are! It is in becoming God-focused and God-centered that we will experience freedom.

Three More Lists: Fears, Secrets, Those We've Hurt

Our work isn't finished, although we've made a good start. We should find three more sheets of paper and compile three more lists after we have worked on our wounds list. The first list is simple: a list of our fears. Many of our fears have likely emerged in the "our part" column of the wounds list, but some may not have. Our fears can often be difficult to identify because we avoid thinking about them and spend significant time building up lives that prevent our fears from being triggered. Remember, when I say "F.E.A.R.," I mean "Future Events Appearing Real." For example, our fears may include not having enough money, not being successful, being unattractive, not being likable or lovable, being alone, or dying. We need to write these fears down on paper so that we can see them once and for all. Fear is a subtle foe. I genuinely believe that many of us are fundamentally motivated by deeply seated fears. It often takes time and the help of someone outside of us looking in, but if we're humble and honest, we can identify fear at work in a significant number of our choices every day. Sometimes fear can manifest itself bodily (e.g., stomachaches, headaches, shakiness, tightening chest), but sometimes it's more cognitive (e.g., racing thoughts, thoughts of dread, etc.).

Steps Three and Four

Either way, take time to sit with yourself and recognize any of these thoughts or bodily sensations. Allow them to indicate for you where there may be fear present.

The second sheet of paper should contain our deepest secrets. The things that cause us shame, but that we have not shared with anyone. The saying goes, "You're as sick as your secrets." So, we have to bring these areas of shame out of the dark and into the light if we are to be free. Our secrets create shame and shame shackles us. We spend time trying to hide our shame or avoid people, places, and things that activate our shame. Carl Jung once wrote, "People will do anything, no matter how absurd, in order to avoid facing their own souls. One does not become enlightened by imagining figures of light, but by making the darkness conscious."[1] If we pretend we are good or imagine we are creatures of light simply because we avoid taking an honest look at ourselves, then we are not free. We need to bring our deep and shameful experiences and secrets into the light.

The final sheet of paper should contain a list of all of the people in our life that we have harmed. Looking at our wounds sheet can be a good starting place. If we look at the column that identifies our part in the situation, we can oftentimes see where we have harmed others, even in small ways, in our attempt to preserve ourselves. Now, admitting that we have hurt or harmed someone does not mean or suggest that we are primarily or predominantly responsible for the situation. It simply means we are taking full responsibility of *our part*. If we are only 1 percent wrong and the other person is 99 percent wrong, then we should still own 100 percent of our 1 percent. That is the purpose of this list—to acknowledge

---

[1] Carl Jung, *Psychology and Alchemy*, vol. 12 of *C. G. Jung: The Collected Works*, ed. Sir Herbert Read, Michael Fordham, and Gerhard Adler, trans. R. F. C. Hull, 2nd ed. (New York: Routledge, 1968), 99.

the harms, no matter how small, that we have caused others through mean words, gossip, slander, stealing, lying, anger, greed, fear, self-interest, and the like.

STEP FOUR: Share my defects of character with myself, another person, and God.

Scripture for Meditation: "Therefore confess your sins to one another, and pray for one another, that you may be healed" (Jas 5:16).

Virtue: Hope

The next step is short, but now that we have our lists, step four requires that we share these lists with another person. The concrete action for step four is to find a sympathetic, compassionate, and trustworthy person to whom we can read our lists out loud. We must admit our character defects to them, to ourselves, and to God. This act of confession is crucial (remember the Fury of confession?).

This step invites us to practice the virtue of hope. Hope is not wishful thinking. Hope is certain. With the virtue of hope, our eyes are directed to heaven, and we are able to live heavenly promises today. Hope allows us to remember God's promise that these barriers won't be with us forever: "He will wipe away every tear from their eyes, and death shall be no more, neither shall there be mourning nor crying nor pain any more, for the former things have passed away" (Rev 21:4). By confessing these defects and shortcomings to the Lord, we're giving Him everything that separates us from Him and allowing Him to continue His healing mission within us (even if that mission won't be completed until heaven).

As Catholics, we know that a natural person to share this list with is a priest, who can offer the Sacrament of Confession.

Steps Three and Four

Not all priests, however, are going to understand or appreciate the work that you are doing. Some may think that you are being too hard on yourself, too exacting, but we must be as thorough and explicit as we can be. After all, we are interested in freedom, not the appearance of freedom.

It's important as well that the person who we choose to hear this list will not give us a pass on our shortcomings: "Hey, that's not so bad; please, don't be so hard on yourself." We need someone that will see these defects of character, these self-preservation strategies for what they are—spiritual cancer, blocks to the action of the Holy Spirit and the voice of God in our hearts.

Naturally, given the sensitive nature of this list, we must find someone who is profoundly trustworthy and mature enough to hold our deep secrets. This is very important. It can be incredibly wounding to share our lists with someone who is not spiritually and emotionally mature enough to handle these parts of ourselves. So, we should not take lightly the task of finding someone whom we have absolute trust in. This is why a good priest will be invaluable if you can find one. We want to walk freely before God and our fellow man. In order to do this we must not hold anything back in this step. We must admit, with open eyes, to ourselves, who and what we are, what we've thought, how we've acted and reacted. We must admit this not only within our own hearts, but to another person, and ultimately before God.

After discussing our character shortcomings with another person, we should take time in quiet to look over our shortcomings. We now see plainly how our selfishness, our ego, and our self-preservation have cut us off from God's grace and God's service. We were serving ourselves and not God. Upon looking at our list, we should pray something like this following prayer adapted from The Big Book of Alcoholics Anonymous: "Loving God, I give myself to you now, completely—all of me, my gift and talents as well as my defects. Please take away any shortcoming that gets in the way of me servicing you and others. I want to do your will, Lord. Give me what I need to do it! Amen."

What loving Father would ask His child to do a task, but not give her what she needs to get it done? What loving Father would give His child a job to do, but not remove the obstacles that prevent His child from doing it? We are called to love and serve God and our fellow man. If we commit ourselves to serving our Heavenly Father, doing His will for us, then He will remove whatever character defects stand in our way of being of service. All that is required is a sincere desire to serve Him and a total surrender of ourselves to Him. The caveat is, however, that we understand that the removal of these defects is for the purpose of serving God, not serving ourselves. The great paradox is that if we turn our hearts away from our sole mission of loving and serving God and our fellow man, many times our defects come roaring back.

Many who have taken this step feel a sense of immediate relief. They are not pretending, hiding, or avoiding anymore. They have faced the hard parts of their lives, relationships, and behaviors. They are not hanging their heads in shame, but holding their heads high. They begin to feel a sense of freedom as they honestly admit the chains that have kept them bound and ask God to remove them.

Further Action Steps

1. Write down any character defects you possess that surprised you. Were there any self-preservation strategies that you felt particularly ashamed of? Why? What does it mean about you if you have this character shortcoming? Surrender these feelings of shame and

Steps Three and Four

fear to God and make an act of trust that our Lord will use you and your past as part of His perfect plan.

2. After sharing your defects of character with yourself, another person, and God, make an act of total consecration to God. Now that you've identified those things blocking you from Him, give yourself to Him, dedicate all that you are, wholly and unreservedly, to God. You can use your own words—what matters most is that to the best of your ability you intend this dedication to the Lord with all of your heart.

Chapter IX

STEPS FIVE AND SIX

STEP FIVE: Make right the wrongs we have done and the harms we have caused to the best of our ability.

Scripture for Meditation: "First be reconciled to your brother, and then come and offer your gift" (Matt 5:24).

Virtue: Justice

We've identified our character defects and admitted them to ourselves, another person, and to God. If we have done this thoroughly and courageously, we've come a long way, but we still aren't quite finished.

Now we must make right the wrongs of the past, so that we can be truly free—in the debt of no one but God.

The concrete action step for step five is to look at the "our part" column of the wounds sheet, as well as the list of people we have harmed. Where have we done wrong? Where have we harmed others? We must now do what we can to right those wrongs.

This is the step of reparation. Through a proportionate response, we need to alleviate the harms and wounds caused by us due to our own defects and spiritual sickness. If we do not try to make right our wrongs then 1) others remain hurt and the cycle continues because they harm others due to the self-preservation we've activated in them (our amends have the power to potentially stop this cycle), and 2) we are not yet fully free because we owe others some good that we've deprived them.

That is why the virtue associated with this step is justice. Justice requires that we give to each person what they are due. In harming someone, we have deprived them or damaged something that they were due. We need to restore justice in our relationships, where it is appropriate to do so, in order to walk freely. Even if we are only 2 percent wrong, we must own 100 percent of our 2 percent. In this case, a simple sorry is not sufficient. Sorry is a mere word. We are after genuine amendment. We are trying to actually make right the wrong, not just cover it over with words. So, if we have stolen money, we do what we can to repay the money. If we have been wasteful with someone else's money, we do what we can to repay them the misspent money. If we have stolen or damaged property, we replace it or compensate the owner for its value. If we've yelled at someone, we attempt to speak with calmness and compassion. Did we harm someone through being manipulative or controlling? We acknowledge this to them and ask how we can make it right.

Remember the five Furies? When we've violated our conscience by depriving someone of a good their owed, we must engage in atonement. We must pay the debt we owe them or else we will find our conscience trying to assuage itself in all sorts of less-than-helpful ways. This step is also about

Steps Five and Six

reconciliation, though. We are healing relationships that we have harmed through our actions.

Now, when I say that we are healing relationships, I do not mean that every act of reparation or atonement needs to re-establish relations with the person harmed. It may be that the other person is toxic, abusive, or otherwise incapable of being in a healthy relationship. Regardless, by our act of atonement we amend the brokenness that *we* brought to the relationship, so that the relationship can end without us owing any debt. We clean up the dirt that we contributed to the relationship. Reconciliation doesn't mean the relationship resumes. It merely means that I am now in good standing with this individual, having acknowledged what I've done wrong and done what I can to make it up to them.

How should we go about doing this task? Well, we should keep in mind first that the purpose of this task is not to unburden ourselves—that would be a selfish and self-serving motive. It would just be more avoiding pain. This step is about others. So, a few principles to help us undertake this step rightly:

First, our atonement should be commensurate with the harm done. If we've destroyed someone's property, let's say crashing their car, then we should not offer them fifty dollars. We should seek to compensate them to the degree and in a manner similar to the harm we've done.

Second, we should not shirk this step just because it may be embarrassing or uncomfortable. To those people whom we can make amends, we should, unless making an amends would make the situation worse for the other person or put us in danger of bodily harm. It will be helpful to have a trusted, wise confidant with whom we can discuss whether it is prudent to make reparation to a person.

Third, for some atonement, we may not know what to do to make up for the harm we've caused. We can approach the person, acknowledge the harm we've done them, and say something like, "I know that I wronged you in this way. Is there anything I can do to make it right?" In this way, we invite the person to share what might be meaningful reparation.

Last, there may be some individuals whom we cannot contact, who have passed away, or to whom we should not make some gesture of atonement. In such cases we should cultivate in ourselves a willingness to make things right, should the opportunity arise, and we should engage in living reparation. By living reparation or living atonement, I mean that we should live, from this moment forward, in a way that tries to make right the wrong we have done to this person. We make a firm amendment of our will to act in a way contrary to the way that caused harm to the person. In some cases, we may only have recourse to praying, fasting, or giving alms to some organization relevant to the harm we've caused.

Let's give an example. Say a young, relatively recent college graduate hooked up with a coed one night at a party. He was manipulative and used the young woman only for his own sexual gratification. He realizes this a few years after college, but he no longer has any means of contacting the young woman. He should, in this case, make a living amends, which would involve a commitment to not hook up with or use women in selfish ways. He would commit to treating women with dignity and respect and not as sexual objects. He might even donate money to provide someone a scholarship to a theology of the body conference. This is an example of what a living amends might look like.

In many cases, when we ask others what we can do to make up for the wrongs we've done them, they will say, "Nothing." That's okay, The mere acknowledgement of the harm is sufficient in this case. The key with this step is to be able to ultimately hold our head high in front of all people. We will know after we've finished this step that we have done whatever we could within our reasonable power to make right all the wrongs we've committed. We can stand proudly before others having swept our side of the street clean, so to speak. We will not feel the sting of shame or guilt because we have sought justice in all of our dealings.

This step may take time. It does not need to be done in one day or even in one week. We shouldn't intentionally drag our feet, but this step can organically unfold over months or even years. The key is being honest with ourselves. We should ask ourselves, "Am I stalling because of fear, pride, or shame?"

STEP SIX: Each day turn your thoughts and actions singularly to being of service to God and your neighbors.

Scripture for Meditation: "For you were called to freedom, brethren; only do not use your freedom as an opportunity for the flesh, but through love be servants of one another" (Gal 5:13).

Virtue: Charity

On to the sixth and final step. In this step, we must dedicate our lives each day to serving God and others, to using our newfound freedom to honor God and to carry His will into all of our dealings. After all, is that not the purpose for which we've been healed? We have been healed so that we might be free to do God's will in each and every situation of our life.

As I noted in the beginning of the book, this program demands a major conversion, a change of heart. The completion of one's healing is not simply a sense of emotional ease or comfort, but a daily commissioning, a sending forth into the world to do God's will. Our healing will not be lasting unless we are willing to turn our mind and our hearts, to the best of our ability, to the purpose of serving God and serving others.

Prior to these steps, we awoke in the morning with all

manner of things we had to do on our mind: work, school, jobs, kids, classes, relationships; then if we were lucky we would utter a quick prayer and ask God to bless our efforts. What, you might ask, are the actions associated with the sixth step? Well, now, having worked the prior steps, the first thing we do when we arise is pledge ourselves, that is, consecrate ourselves to the Lord that we might seek only to do His will today. We ask the Lord to remove all of the barriers to hearing His voice and following the promptings of the Holy Spirit. We ask God to remove the various self-preservation habits and fears that cloud our vision and make us ineffective instruments. We might end this period of daily morning prayer with the Prayer of St. Francis. Once we've concluded this period of prayer, we can think about all of the things that we want to accomplish or that are on our "to-do" list with a sense of confidence that we will be able to consider them more accurately now, with the help of God's grace, free from our defects of character and fears. We will have greater clarity about these situations because we will be trying to see with God's eyes and heart, rather than our own.

Human beings are creatures that need goals. Every time we act it is with some end or goal in mind. Until now, many of us have been acting and aiming at goals that are out of order. There is one primary goal: loving and serving God and our fellow man. Jesus tells His disciples, "But seek first [God's] kingdom and his righteousness, and all these things shall be yours as well" (Matt 6:33). What are "these things" that Jesus is speaking of? Just prior to His instruction regarding the kingdom, Jesus is telling His disciples not to worry about what they will eat or drink or wear. He's talking about the first level of the six S's! We need to listen to Jesus and put first things first. If we aim each moment at the first thing—loving and serving God and our fellow man—then everything else falls into place.

Steps Five and Six

How do we seek this kingdom of God? Discussing the nature of the kingdom of God, St. John Paul II writes, "The kingdom aims at transforming human relationships; it grows gradually as people slowly learn to love, forgive and serve one another.... The kingdom's nature, therefore, is one of communion among all human beings—with one another and with God."[2] We seek the kingdom through freely loving, serving, and forgiving one another. We seek the kingdom as we strive for unity and communion with our fellow man. If we're feeling wrecked by our character defects, we should help someone. Anyone. Find someone to serve as an act of love to God and the person. This is seeking the kingdom.

The virtue associated with this step is the virtue of charity: to love God and to love our neighbors in God. Living a life of charity is the height of holiness. It is the purpose of our lives. In this final step, the virtue of charity is encouraged to bloom and blossom each day for the rest of our life.

We should not assume that simply praying in the morning is sufficient. We must build the habit of asking God many times during the day to reveal His will to us, to show us the course of action to take. Undoubtedly, we will have moments of confusion, indecision, and uncertainty. In these moments we should pause and ask God to give us an inspiration or insight into His will for us. Our new goal is not self-preservation, but service—God-oriented service, not self-oriented service. We must decrease, so that He can increase (see John 3:30). As we are purified of our defects of character and our fears, we will become better lovers—better lovers of God and better lovers of our fellow man.

---

[2] Pope St. John Paul II, Encyclical on the Permanent Validity of the Church's Missionary Mandate *Redemptoris Missio* (December 7, 1990), §15.

In the course of our day, we should look for ways to get out of "self" and into service. If we cannot be helpful in a situation, we should be mindful not to make a situation worse. In this way, we will be reducing the likelihood of experiencing (or causing) secondary wounds. Throughout the day, as we notice our self-preservation strategies flare up. It can be helpful to remember H.A.L.T.S. (hungry, angry, lonely, tired, and scared). Our preservations strategies are more likely to emerge in one of these conditions. Regardless of the conditions in which they arise, it is important to notice them, name them, ask God to remove them, and then ask God what He wants you to do in a given situation. In this way, we might be the most effective instruments of His will. Allowing defects an opportunity to grow will only cost us secondary wounds and prevent us from experiencing the sense of purpose and meaning found in the will of God.

When we were concerned with self-preservation, life felt hard. We spent significant energy and time pursuing our own ends. It was a bit like walking upstream in a river. Now, as we radically and daily turn our minds and hearts to God, we find a greater sense of ease. It is not perfect calm all the time; it's more like floating down a river. Sure, there are rapids and bumps and splashing water, but we expend much less energy and effort than when we were paddling upstream. We allow the will of God to flow in and through us, and in doing so we find ourselves meeting people, seeing places, and having experiences that we never thought that we might have.

Further Action Steps

1. Sometimes we still experience feelings of resentment and anger at someone for something they may have done to us, even after we acknowledge our part and reframe their behavior as ultimately a form of spiritual

Steps Five and Six

sickness (e.g., disconnection from God's love, peace, and security). If there are still individuals toward whom you feel angry, resentful, or bitter, acknowledge that fact honesty and begin by praying for them daily for two weeks. Pray for them everything that you desire for yourself (e.g., health, peace, family unity, love, etc.). Even if you don't mean the words with your heart, simply be faithful to saying the words. Pray for them until you start to genuinely mean the words you are praying.

2. In what ways can you seek to be of service to God and others in the midst of your unchanging duties and responsibilities (i.e., work, parenting, school, religious vocation)?

3. Are there particular times that you tend to notice your defects of character pop up (e.g., at night, at work, etc.)? Why do you think that is? What can you do to reduce the likelihood that you will act on your defects during these times?

Chapter X

RESTORED IN CHRIST—
HEALING IN THE SACRAMENTS

A Healing Touch

In a number of Christ's physical healings the Gospels make a point of highlighting that Jesus touches the person He heals. In the Gospel of Mark Jesus heals the blind man by mixing His spit with dirt and putting the resulting mud on the man's eyes (Mark 8:23). He touches the man's eyes as He covers his blindness with the mixture of spit and dirt. In the Gospel of Luke Jesus heals a woman who is bent over. We're told that He does this by touching her: "When Jesus saw her, he called her over and said to her, 'Woman, you are freed from your infirmity.' And he laid his hands upon her, and immediately she was made straight, and she praised God" (Luke 13:12-13). The touch of Christ is healing.

Yet, it's not only when Christ reaches out to touch us that we are healed. In His mercy, even when we reach out in desperation and doubt healing occurs. Recall the story of the hemorrhaging woman. She merely touches the hem of His garment and she is made well (Luke 8:43–48). Or consider St. Thomas the Apostle. Thomas reaches out and touches Christ. He sticks his finger into Christ's wound and his doubt is healed: "Upon him was the chastisement that made us whole, and with his stripes we are healed" (Isa 53:5–6). Christ's wounds are the vestiges of the Cross, the signs of His profound love for us. We are healed by the Cross. We are healed by God's love. This is why the cover art on the book is St. Thomas touching the wound of Christ. Christ's wounds are the tangible signs of His love for us. They are the visible marks of His healing mission. If there were any question whether the Lord wants to heal us, we need only look at His wounds. Christ invites us, like the Apostle Thomas, into His wounds so that in them we might touch His love and be healed.

After working our way through the steps, we have identified the barriers to deeper, life-giving union with Christ. We've seen the parts of self that block us from a love that can heal and that frees us. We've looked at the fear, the distorted thought patterns, the behaviors, the manifestations of self-preservation, and the grudges that have kept us in bondage—living a life in reaction to our wounds. We've invited Christ into our wounds and asked Him to remove the obstacles that are preventing us from being of service to Him. The Lord is obsessed with our freedom. From the proto-evangelium to the Israelites' captivity in Egypt and the wandering in the desert; from the judges, who continually rescued their people, to Christ, the literal embodiment of our liberation, God's mission has been one of healing and freedom. We will find that God will give us the freedom we desire in order to serve Him. He will provide the healing we so desperately seek. We will also find that as we begin to experience this healing, our experience of the sacraments will change—particularly the Eucharist and Confession.

This new encounter with Christ in the sacraments will deepen our healing.

The Eucharist

Until now, we've been receiving the Eucharist while maintaining and persisting in our self-preservation strategies. The problem is, we do not perceive or experience love accurately or fully when it is viewed through the pain of our wounds or the comfort of our self-preservation. Our character defects create a barrier, so to speak, from the touch that Christ offers in the Eucharist. Our ego, our self-righteousness, our grudges, our fears of vulnerability, our sense that we are not lovable, all distort our experience of Christ in the Eucharist. They block the full force of His touch.

Through the steps, we have begun to work on our image of God and to clear away the various aspects of self that prevent us from freely following the voice and will of God. From this place of humility, genuineness, and authenticity, when we receive the Eucharist now, we can actually begin to experience God as He really is—good. Remember the line in the *Catechism* that suggested that all sin—all of the unhealthy expressions of self, self-seeking, ego, and the rest—arose from not trusting that God is good (CCC 397)? Well, as we remove the barriers of self that have been cutting us off from the light and grace of the Spirit, we can begin to actually experience God as good. Nowhere more so than in the Eucharist. To touch and be touched by Christ in the Eucharist heals our misperceptions of God and sets us on the road to ever-deepening love and freedom.

Once we tap into the power of Christ's love in the Eucharist, we will experience a dynamic and unpredictable journey. Since it is ultimately Christ's love that heals, He will, over time, help us discover and uncover all of the ways that we continue to remain distant from Him, bound by our own egos, and slaves to self-preservation and sin. He will direct the journey of healing, as long as we stay connected to Him, most especially through the Eucharist. He will reveal, in His time, those areas of our life that need attention, the parts of life we were not spiritually mature enough to address earlier, those subtle ways that we give ourselves passes on certain bad habits, and those vices that we have actually pretended were virtues. In His love we will see ourselves more clearly, and be willing and able to take the risk to be honest and vulnerable in acknowledging our need to continually grow. We must steep ourselves every day, every minute in His profound love for us. We must allow this love to penetrate and permeate our being. Christ's love for us must become the motivator for all things—from this place of love, what am I called to do? How am I called to act? In His love, the fortresses of self that we have constructed will be slowly deconstructed over and over, time and again, until the humble and loving Christ stands guard: "He must increase, but I must decrease" (John 3:30).

I'm reminded of an image received in prayer that a friend shared with me. She recounted how in this prayer she viewed herself as a castle. Her wounds were gaping holes or breaches in the castle wall. She noted that in the original image she received, she stood guard at the breach in the castle wall. She knew that she was not able to guard herself adequately against all of life's hurts and attacks, which made guarding the hole in the wall exhausting and terrifying. In the midst of this prayer, however, Our Lord gave her a new image. He revealed to her that He wanted to stand guard in all of His radiance and love at the hole in the castle's wall—in her hurts and wounds. He wanted to relieve her from the exhausting work of trying to protect herself. This is a beautiful and helpful image as we imagine how Christ deepens our healing in the Eucharist. With each reception, His love replaces our defenses and frees us to be transformed by Him. In the love and security found in our deepened faith we are able to live in the freedom of beloved sons and daughters of God.

The Eucharist Heals Our Memories

When, throughout life, we are tempted to forget who we are, when our sinfulness and our wounds seem to overwhelm us, and when we feel trapped in the prison of self, the Eucharist serves as a reminder of our identity. In a homily given on the Feast of Corpus Christi Pope Francis reflects beautifully on this theme. In his homily he says,

> So many people have memories marked by a lack of affection and bitter disappointments caused by those who should have given them love and instead orphaned their hearts. . . . God, however, can heal these wounds by placing within our memory a greater love: his own love. The Eucharist brings us the Father's faithful love, which heals our sense of being orphans. . . . It fills our hearts with the consoling love of the Holy Spirit, who never leaves us alone and always heals our wounds.[1]

Reception of the Eucharist reminds us of who we are at our core—we are the Father's beloved creations. We are not lost or forgotten, unmoored in life. Rather, we are redeemed in love by the Father, finding our home in His loving heart. The pope goes on in the same homily to suggest that the Eucharist can also heal our negative memories:

---

[1] Pope Francis, Homily on the Feast of Corpus Christi (June 14, 2020), https://www.catholicnewsagency.com/news/44855/full-text-pope-francis-corpus-christi-homily.

> The Lord knows that evil and sins do not define us; they are diseases, infections. And he comes to heal them with the Eucharist, which contains the antibodies to our negative memory. With Jesus, we can *become immune to sadness* [emphasis mine]. We will always remember our failures, troubles, problems at home and at work, our unrealized dreams. But their weight will not crush us because Jesus is present even more deeply, encouraging us with his love.

Here, the pope suggests that the love we encounter in the Eucharist inoculates us against the sadness and despair that often accompany us, knowing just how sinful, selfish, and broken we are. The Eucharist serves as a reminder that His love for us swallows in its very immensity our woundedness and our troubles. Finally, the pope states that the Eucharist can break us out of the prison of self that binds us. He says,

> For only love can heal fear at its root and free us from the self-centeredness that imprisons us. And that is what Jesus does. He approaches us gently, in the disarming simplicity of the Host. He comes as Bread broken in order to break open the shells of our selfishness. He gives of himself in order to teach us that only by opening our hearts can we be set free from our interior barriers, from the paralysis of the heart.

The love of God calls us out of our self-centeredness and self-sufficiency. God's love provides a deep security that allows us to risk letting go of our old habits, ideas, and behaviors. Because of our pasts, many of us grow hypersensitive to interpersonal threats—we are constantly on guard for the threat that someone might wound us. In the Eucharist, however, Christ comes in humility and love. He does not approach us as a threat, but in a gentleness that invites us to let go of our defenses that we might be healed. In so doing, "The Eucharist received with love and adored with fervor becomes a school of freedom and charity in order to fulfil the commandment to love."[2]

Confession

It is not only the Eucharist, however, that will aid in our subsequent healing. The Sacrament of Confession may take on a new and more profound significance as we work our steps as well. With our new knowledge of the causes and conditions of many of our problems, we can begin to confess the roots of the sin rather than just the sinful fruit. The grace of forgiveness can touch the deepest parts of our sin and therefore bring about greater healing.

As our concern for self-preservation decreases, we will be less fearful of admitting our wrongs and more desirous of the love and grace found in forgiveness. Confession will become a welcome avenue for reflection, growth, humility, and healing. Where once we were afraid of the Sacrament of Confession, we now begin to look forward to admitting our faults, for this is a crucial part of remaining free.

While we certainly will not be approaching the Sacrament of Confession daily, we should be confessing our shortcomings and failings to ourselves, God, and another trusted friend on a daily basis, especially when our misdeed is serious or particularly shameful. We must not resort to trying to present a false image of ourselves. Spiritual progress and healing demand that we be honest with ourselves and others.

---

[2] Pope St. John Paul II, Message of the Holy Father John Paul II to the Youth of the World on the Occasion of the XIX World Youth Day (April 4, 2004), §5, https://www.vatican.va/content/john-paul-ii/en/messages/youth/documents/hf_jp-ii_mes_20040301_xix-world-youth-day.html.

On our healing journey we should try to develop a regular habit of attending the Sacrament of Confession. In this sacrament, we will be renewing the humility that helps us to feel peaceful, calm, and detached. A good confession will require that we are honest about who and how we are. We will unashamedly see that we are in desperate need of God's help and grace. In this humility, we will be more likely to identify, acknowledge, and let go of all of the ways that we pursue our own program of happiness apart from the Lord's love and guidance.

Confession will also allow us to make a habit of uncovering those secrets which keep us enslaved to shame. In Confession we honestly acknowledge those dark parts of ourselves that we have spent considerable effort hiding from ourselves and others. As we practice this honesty, we will find ourselves better able to communicate sincerity and authenticity in our affairs.

Receiving the Sacraments of the Eucharist and Confession in conjunction with these steps can allow us to encounter the love of God in a new and profound way. We will be renewed and restored in Christ. We will find in Him the freedom and healing that He desires for us. We will be drawn into a love affair with our Savior—the one who is trustworthy and good.

The Sacramentality of Life

As we heal, we also begin to see God in and through creation. We see God's presence in more and more of the circumstances, encounters, and relationships that we experience. Where we were once blinded by our own fear, self-seeking, and insecurities, we now see God's gentle hand providentially and lovingly guiding us.

This does not mean that everything will be roses. On the contrary, we will still suffer, perhaps greatly. Our suffering may be confusing, frustrating, and difficult to bear. There are sufferings so troubling that they cloud or blot out the vision of God's presence in our lives. Some sufferings are so profound that we feel paralyzed by grief and the perceived absence of God's presence: "My God, my God, why have you forsaken me?" (Matt 27:46). In such cases we do not see God in our experiences. Yet, Christ has already gone to that place. From the Cross He shows us that He has entered that darkness and abandonment. He knows it. He waits for us there. He has conquered it.

Without the impediments of our old habits, ideas, and behaviors, we are much less likely to make things worse, to respond to our suffering in unhealthy and harmful ways. We can have the courage, patience, and trust to accept rather than fight our suffering. This is not the resignation of the defeated, but the humble trust of a child. In these moments of darkness, we must ask the Lord for the patience, strength, and courage to endure our difficulties. We should ask the Lord, from the depths of our deepest trials and sufferings, what it is that He wants for each of us, as unique creations and beloved children. We can sit with the Lord in this darkness and wait on Him. Sometimes He illuminates the darkness; sometimes He holds us in our distress, anguish, and inability to understand until the tidal wave of suffering dissipates.

Concluding Thoughts

There is a reciprocal relationship between our healing and the sacraments. Engaging in our own journey of healing frees us to experience the sacraments in a new and more profound way. In the absence of the various ways that we turn away from God to pursue our own wills, our own preservation, or our own satisfaction, we are more likely to experience the dynamic and powerful touch of Christ. Yet, in this touch, we are given the grace to further our healing journey. We receive strength, courage, and wisdom to approach emotional and spiritual barriers that were previously unknown or too scary. We have a divine companion, Love Itself, to help us hold our sufferings and primary wounds. Put in other terms, our work with these steps better disposes us to receive the graces of the sacraments, and in receiving these graces, we are drawn into deeper union with Christ—into greater healing and freedom.

Questions for Reflection

1. Listen closely to the words of absolution after your next confession. After admitting all of your defects of character, your deepest secrets and fears, and making your amends to others, what do you think and feel when you hear these words?

2. Since working these steps, have you noticed any differences in your experience of the Mass, the Eucharist, or Confession? It's okay if the answer is no. It can take time for our experience to change and sometimes it's a miracle just to make it through a Mass (e.g., you have a bunch of kiddos). Occasionally check in with your experience of the sacraments to see if you notice any differences.

Prayer

Father, you do not leave us orphans, alone in our suffering and pain. Instead You draw near to us. Through the sacraments you touch us with Your love. Help us to see and feel Your healing love in the Eucharist and Confession. Draw us deeper into Your wounds, for by Your stripes we are healed. Amen.

Chapter XI

ONE DAY AT A TIME

PERHAPS THROUGH THE COURSE of the steps, you have experienced the profound removal of your defects of character and their effects. Where once there was anxiety, fear, anger, greed, procrastination, a hardened heart toward a family member, now there is faith, peace, service, diligence, and love. If this is the case, then your freedom must be used in an effort of being the most effective instrument of love to God and your fellow man that you can be.

Maybe your healing is more like that of St. Paul. You may not have experienced a profound removal of your defects of character or their effects in every area of your life, but instead you've been given the tools to name them, identify how they get you in trouble, and ask God to remove them from being a barrier to doing His will. We can still keep our thorns and be free to love God and serve our fellow man. Despite our thorns, we will find great meaning and purpose in being attentive to God's call each moment of our life. We will be free. God will use our thorns and struggles to serve Him and others. We will see how our experiences will become fountains of healing for those that God deigns us to encounter. We must remain open—each day, each moment. We have a new focus and purpose—maximum service to God and others.

The End Game

Ultimately, these steps are really about re-establishing a new and profound relationship with God. They are about *metanoia*—turning our hearts fully back to God. Another way of saying this: these steps are about daily conversion. What was in our way? We were.

As we recognize the various and subtle forms of selfishness that pervade our lives and seek remove them, we become better at loving; we become receptive of the Holy Spirit, and docile to God's will. This is holiness. We are able to get out of God's way, so that we can live the life He has in store for us. We remove our ego (Latin for "I"; but as an acronym, "E.G.O." is "Edge God Out"). Where we used to edge God out and fill ourselves with various forms of self, we now seek to carve out our unhealthy selfishness and fill ourselves with a relationship with God.

In a training video[1] regarding a therapy she developed, Dr. Sue Johnson said, "Freud was wrong. Sex and aggression are not the most powerful instincts in man. The most powerful instinct in man is his or her need to connect with another human being. To call out into the darkness and hugeness of life and say, 'Are you there?' And to get an answer: 'Yes, I'm there. I'm with you. You are not alone in the universe.' That answer changes everything." See, these steps are about

---

[1] Sue Johnson, "Emotionally Focused Individual Therapy (EFIT): Attachment-Based Interventions to Treat Trauma, Anxiety, and Depression," *PESI Training Video*.

removing the barriers of ego and self that prevent you from hearing and experiencing God's response, "Yes, I'm here. I'm with you. You are not alone." The more we hear this and feel this in our very being, the more secure we will feel in God, in ourselves, and in the world. We will not need self-preservation strategies or to satisfy our egos because we will have security and fulfillment in God.

Now some people may still be struggling to a degree that requires help from a counselor or therapist. That is okay! These steps should still be of aid to you. Even if we are still struggling with past trauma, clinical depression, or clinical anxiety, these steps can be an aid to us in clearing away the parts of ourselves that are making our psychological difficulties harder to endure. For example, where do we have false beliefs or fears about how our psychological struggles are going to affect our lives? Are we having a difficult time accepting aspects of our struggles because of our various self-preservation strategies? We should not be afraid or ashamed to see a therapist or counselor for help and support. Nor should we eschew medication if it is prescribed by a competent psychiatrist. If one is still struggling after working these steps, hopefully the steps have helped clear away any false beliefs or barriers preventing you from seeking the further psychological help you need. As we've grown in humility, courage, love, and self-knowledge throughout the steps, none of our activities should have exacerbated our problems; instead, we now have a more robust relationship with our loving God, and in this, have greater access to His peace and power, even in emotional or psychological struggles.

The process of healing and growing spiritually will take time. It is a lifetime endeavor. We begin again anew each day. As we conclude, I want to bring to your attention four actions that should accompany us throughout each day as we live this daily conversion. None of these are merely to be intellectually pondered. They must be lived.

Prayer

In order to be of service to God and man we *must* begin each day in prayer. Prayer will become our time to receive our marching orders, so to speak. It will be our time to tap into the stream of power and grace that will guide and direct the flow of our day. It's our moment to bathe ourselves in the sunlight of the Holy Spirit in order to nourish our interior lives. In prayer we tap into the wellspring that will allow us to live in the freedom of God's grace and guidance. Fr. Jacques Philippe captures nicely the process of turning inward to find this wellspring:

> When a person is faithful to his or her times of prayer, day after day, week after week, it's like someone with a well in the garden that's choked with rubbish—branches, leaves, stones, mud—but underneath is water, clean and pure. In spending time in prayer, you're setting to work to unblock the well. What comes up at the start is the mud and dirt: our wretchedness, worries, fears, guilt, self-blame—the things we normally avoid. Plenty of people run away from themselves. There's a real fear of silence today! But those who have the courage to go forward into the desert end up finding an oasis.[2]

Prayer is indispensable—a must—in clearing away the parts of self that are choking our garden. In addition to the steps, fidelity to prayer will increase God's life and light in us, helping us

---

[2] Fr. Jacques Philippe, "Trusting More and More," chap. 4 in *The Way of Trust and Love* (New York: Scepter Publishers, 2012).

to see our selfishness and the self-preservation that block us from the wellspring. Our steps help us clear away blocks to the wellspring, but we must use prayer to begin to drink from the spring. Fr. Philippe concludes, "by going to the depths of our hearts in prayer we find pure, clear water. . . . But the only things that give us access to the depths of our hearts, to our deepest identity, to the child of God that each of us is, are faith and prayer."

We should begin our day with a simple prayer:

God, I give myself completely to you today.
Ask anything of me. Send me anywhere today
to do anything.
I only ask that you take away the ways that my selfishness,
self-preservation, and ego get in my way of
serving you and others.
Make my day and my life a sign to everyone I encounter
of your love, power, and peace.

You might also pray the Prayer of St. Francis. We are, after all, trying to be beacons of God's life, love, and peace—serving others rather than serving ourselves by seeking our security. Spend some time quietly listening to anything God might be saying in the depths of your heart. This period of listening can be short—three to five minutes. Perhaps you hear some word, inspiration, or have some intuition. Perhaps you don't. The point is to place yourself in God's presence and open yourself up to receiving whatever He may have for you. We should try to carry God's presence with us throughout our day, asking for His guidance, insight, intuition, and help when we are confused, stuck, or unsure. At the end of the day we should find a good examination of conscience and spend time reviewing our day, seeing where we may owe restitution, asking for help in areas where we might improve, and resting in the love of our God.

Gratitude

Many of us are in the habit of thinking negatively. We have what is called a negativity bias. We are really good at seeing threat, danger, what's wrong, what might go wrong, what could be better. This way of thinking is like second nature for many of us. So, if we are to combat negativity bias, we need to start practicing gratitude daily. To build this habit, start the day off with three things that you are genuinely grateful for from the previous day. At the end of each day spend time considering three things you are grateful for from the day. Your gratitude list doesn't have to have big things on it. It can have small things you're grateful for (e.g., five minutes to drink coffee and call my best friend, a good mechanic whom I trust, having an uninterrupted seven hours of sleep last night). By practicing a gratitude list we will be practicing seeing the positive in the day and in each situation. We will be combatting our negativity bias.

Forgiveness

When we find ourselves feeling angry or hurt by others (and we often will), we use what we have learned through the steps about ourselves to begin the process of forgiveness. When hurt by someone, we try to see how it is really their self-preservation strategies that have harmed us. It's their defects of character that we dislike, and though we certainly don't like how they've harmed us, we sure do understand. Having seen our own defects of character and admitted how we've harmed others, we now begin to have some compassion for others. We've not been wounded by a whole and happy person, but by someone who is spiritually sick, like we once were—someone who is cut off from the freedom in the Holy

Spirit. We have been hurt by someone who is trying to keep themselves feeling safe and secure. It doesn't justify their actions, but we can begin to understand them. When we can put ourselves into another's shoes we start to empathize and begin to forgive, and forgive we must (see Matt 18:22).

Acceptance

Many of us have struggled with control. We want life to proceed the way we want. We've spent time, effort, and energy trying to change and manipulate situations that are beyond our control. We tried to make life as we would have it be—after our image and our likeness—precisely because we struggled with acceptance. Accepting life and the people in it as they are rather than as we would have them be is essential to our peace and happiness. When we were acting out of our character defects and fear, we could not accept God's will in our lives, because oftentimes God's will didn't fit with our self-preservation strategies or it activated our fears. Now that we've begun to clear away these aspects of ourselves that have been driving us, we can now see more clearly what we have control over and what God is asking us to accept. We can see His will more clearly. We know that we are not in charge and that we must learn to accept unpleasant and unwanted aspects of life and others if we are to have any peace in this life and if we are to be of service to God (as He would have us be, not in the way we want to be). We must also practice accepting the discomfort of our sufferings. We've spent significant effort trying to avoid suffering, yet maturity and healing demand that we practice learning to hold and sit with uncomfortable feelings, thoughts, memories, and bodily sensations. We don't have to reflexively react in ways to reduce them. We can accept these feelings and then consider in light of God's will what He would have us do. This process of accepting suffering without reflexive reaction (e.g., avoiding, distracting, numbing, controlling) takes time and practice, so we need to be patient and gentle with ourselves.

Inviting God into this process, through the following prayer, has helped countless others through the years and I hope it blesses you as well:

> *God, give me grace to accept with serenity*
> *the things that cannot be changed,*
> *Courage to change the things*
> *which should be changed,*
> *and the Wisdom to distinguish*
> *the one from the other.*
> *Living one day at a time,*
> *Enjoying one moment at a time,*
> *Accepting hardship as a pathway to peace,*
> *Taking, as Jesus did,*
> *This sinful world as it is,*
> *Not as I would have it,*
> *Trusting that You will make all things right,*
> *If I surrender to Your will,*
> *So that I may be reasonably happy in this life,*
> *And supremely happy with You forever in the next.*
> *Amen.*

Questions for Reflection

1. What has been your experience of working these steps? What aspects of this program have been significantly impactful or beneficial to you? Why? Were there parts of the program that feel difficult? If so, why?

2. What obstacles will get in the way of you living the principles of this program each day? What concrete action steps can you take to help you remove or diminish these obstacles? What behaviors or changes

are you willing to commit to, in order to make space in your life for this new way of living? Invite God into these impediments. Listen to any inspirations or intuitions as to how the Lord wants you to deal with these obstacles.

APPENDIX A: SOME COMMON QUESTIONS

Is this program enough? I've worked through the steps and I'm still struggling with emotional and psychological pain.

For some people the steps contained in this book may be enough. Other people may need the professional aid of a therapist or counselor to help them work through traumas, traumatic memories, pervasive unhealthy relationship habits, addictions, and so forth. One of the problems with self-guided programs, like the one outlined in this book, is that they rely on our ability to see ourselves clearly and our capacity to be rigorously honest with ourselves. Sometimes, however, we cannot see ourselves as clearly as others see us. We have blind spots—areas in our lives where others see our need for growth and help, but where we see no issue or reason for concern. Another problem with self-guided programs like the one I've outlined is that they are intentionally general in order to capture the experience of as many people and problems as possible. Some folks may need a treatment that really focuses on very particular problems or specific aspects of a person's experience. Therefore, some people may need a trained professional to help them see issues that they have missed or to provide treatments developed to treat very particular emotional problems or life experiences. There is no shame or harm in this. The program outlined in this book can still serve as an aid, even for those in counseling or therapy. Tapping into God's grace in a new and dynamic way oftentimes can aid traditional therapy. If, however, your therapist advises you to put down this book or to not use these steps, then follow the advice of your treatment provider.

Appendix A: Some Common Questions

You're telling me that I'm the problem, but I have been at the receiving end of real abuse that I didn't cause! It sounds to me like you're blaming the victim. How can you tell me that I'm to blame for the hurt that's been done to me?

This is a tough one. It is important to understand that no one deserves abuse. The culpability (moral responsibility) for abuse firmly rests on the abuser and is not shared by the abused. The reason for this is that we have free will. We really are (except in some very specific cases) in control of our actions. That means that no one can *make* or force us to act in one way or another. We choose how we act. Similarly, we cannot cause another person to act in any way. They choose how to act. So, they always bear the blame or moral responsibility for their actions.

It's also important to keep in mind that there are hurts and wounds that we endure in which we have played absolutely no role. We have not created or contributed to the circumstances that precipitated our being wounded.

That being said, where appropriate, applicable, and reasonable, we should look for our part and own it, no matter how small. Many of us default consciously or unconsciously to blaming others rather than assuming responsibility and identifying where we are to blame. By assuming responsibility when it is truly ours, we can empower ourselves. Finding our contribution to a situation allows us to have some power to change our experiences and the circumstances of our lives. We regain a sense of power to shape our lives and our experiences moving forward—we begin to feel less helpless. In looking for our contribution to a situation we are recognizing that while we cannot *cause* anyone to act in certain ways, we can increase the likelihood or probability of someone acting in certain ways toward us. Let's see if an example helps shed some light on this. Imagine someone who is verbally and emotionally abused for years. After taking abuse for so long, the abused person eventually lashes out in physical violence. The abuser didn't cause the abused person to react with violence nor are they morally responsible for the violence itself; however, it seems abundantly clear that the abuser contributed to and created conditions for increasing the likelihood that they might be on the receiving end of violence. Certain conditions are such that people are *more likely* to act or react in unhealthy ways. Sometimes we are responsible for creating these circumstances.

Are you telling me that I can be healed and still be suffering?

Absolutely. In fact, a large part of healing is being able to suffer well. So much of our emotional and psychological pain is caused by trying to avoid, get rid of, or get out of suffering. Being healed means I don't have to avoid suffering. I can experience and hold my pain without making it worse or condemning myself as a failure for suffering. Anxiety, grief, sadness, loneliness, fear—these are all healthy, normal, human feelings, which, when experienced, can feel distressing, unwanted, or like suffering. To be able to hold my anxiety or my sadness and simply experience it, while still pursuing what God is asking of me, is a mark of healing. Remember, healing isn't freedom from suffering; it is freedom to answer God's call in the midst of suffering. I can feel deep loneliness and grief over the loss of a family member and not use all my emotional control strategies and self-preservation to create more pain out of the suffering (e.g., I shouldn't be feeling this way if I have real faith).

Should we make amends to people who are emotionally abusive?

This is a tricky question—one that requires honest prayer, discernment, and the insight from someone who understands these steps and what we are trying to achieve. One thing is

Appendix A: Some Common Questions

clear, we should *never* make amends to a person, business, or institution that is going to put us at risk of physical harm. But what about cases where the person to whom we are going to make amends might respond with verbal abuse? Should we subject ourselves to that abuse? It seems like it depends. What is our motivation for avoiding the amends? Are we acting out of fear? Fear that our feelings will be hurt or fear that the person's response may expose us to feelings that we don't like or find uncomfortable (e.g., anger)? If our motivation is avoidance or fear of having our feelings hurt, then it seems like we should make amends. After all, we do not want to be slaves to fear—we want freedom. It should be noted, however, that *we are not* doormats. We are beloved children of God. We should not let others mistreat us. So, in such cases that someone becomes verbally abusive during an amends, we can say, "I'd like to finish my amends to you, but I cannot continue if you're going to continue speaking to me or treating me like this." If the person calms down, you can continue the amends. If not, you should remove yourself from the situation. A good amends doesn't mean that the person responds well or even accepts the amends. A good amends is about your willingness to keep *your* side of the street clean. Now, if you know that making an amends will infuriate someone else or cause them emotional suffering and pain, then it may be prudent to hold off on the amends. We should not view an amends as the emotional unburdening of yourself at the expense of another—that would just be selfish. If the amends will cause emotional, psychological, or spiritual harm for the other person, we should likely avoid making amends.

Appendix A: Some Common Questions

Let's say I've done something illegal or something for which I could receive serious consequences: Should I make amends and admit what I've done?

Here again, the answer is it depends. We should pray about this and talk it through with a trusted advisor. We should be willing to face the consequences of our actions if it is called for. It's not, however, always called for. For example, if making amends means that you could go to jail for some offense you've committed, you should consider your current situation first. Do you have a family? Would you be harming your children or spouse? Are there people or organizations you have responsibilities to that would be seriously harmed by your absence? As we heal and grow in freedom, we begin to focus more on serving others. We can't always help others, but we can try not to harm others. So, if making an amends will cause significant harm to others, then it may be in the best interests of everyone to make an anonymous amends or a living amends.

Do I have to make amends to someone for something that they don't know I've done?

It depends. If you deprived someone of property, money, or some opportunity, then it may be worthwhile to make amends of some sort to the person even if you're convinced that they may not have known that you wronged them. For example, imagine as a high schooler you used to sneak into a neighbor's garage and steal beer from their refrigerator. Should you make amends, even if the neighbor likely didn't notice one missing beer occasionally? If you think that it would cause more harm than good to the neighbor to confess the wrongdoing, you could certainly just drop off a six-pack (or the equivalent of what you stole) to their house anonymously or perhaps give it as a gift for Christmas. If it wouldn't cause harm to them, you can even share the reason why you are dropping off the beer.

Appendix A: Some Common Questions

Now, in cases where you gossiped or spoke ill of someone to another person it is likely not in anyone's best interest to tell the person that you spoke ill of them to others. Rather than approaching the person you've spoken ill about and confessing this wrongdoing to them (though it should be confessed to someone else in the course of the steps), you might make amends by making a point of going out of your way to be nice to them or deliberately celebrating their gifts to other people.

I understand that these steps ultimately boil down to freeing us to be of service to God and to others and that maintaining our healing requires that we continue to help and serve others, but I feel like I already frequently help others. How can you tell me to keep helping and serving others?

Motivation is key. For many people, helping and serving others is not done in the spirit of doing God's will or selflessness, but it is actually about self-serving motives. Sometimes we need to take a good honest look at *why* we serve others. For some people, they perform acts of service, so that other people will be more likely to help them in the future. We might find ourselves being kind to someone because we think it will benefit us in some way. For others, acts of service help prevent conflict. If I'm always the nice person doing things for other people, I can avoid being in the crosshairs of conflict. Still other people engage in service because it makes them look good. We help others because our peers view us as Good Samaritans. It plays into an image or identity that we want to maintain. We cannot merely look at the behaviors we are engaged in. We must look at our motivations, our heart. We must seek to engage in the right behaviors for the right reasons. Can we serve others for selfless rather than selfish motives? Can we serve with a purer heart? Can we seek to be of maximum service to others, rather than moderately helpful?

Appendix A: Some Common Questions

You've talked a lot about self-preservation and how it is at the root of many of our problems. Is all self-preservation bad?

No. The act of self-preservation is not always bad and not all forms of self-preservation are bad. When our self-preservation clearly hurts someone (i.e., through greed, laziness, self-interest), then it should be identified, rooted out, or avoided, but there are times when self-preservation can be healthy and even necessary. Self-preservation can serve as the buffer or the break that we need in order to respond to a person or situation in a mature manner. Having a larger than average bowl of ice cream after a stressful day can be a perfectly fine response, if it gives you a little break or reset from the stressful day and allows you to return in better form tomorrow. Sometimes we need a break to treat ourselves—to take care of our own needs in order to feel recharged and refreshed. On the surface this might look like, or even feel like, laziness, greed, or self-interest (but it's not). As long as we are not actively harming someone or making this response habitual, then it falls under the category of self-care, and we should not worry. Perhaps some mornings you resort to ice cream for breakfast because you're exhausted, don't feel like cooking, and just need to make it through the morning—you're just trying to survive. Perhaps you binge-watch a TV show some nights. These sorts of self-preservation strategies are fine as long as they don't become your default response to difficulties and they do not seriously injure someone. Avoiding a difficult conversation with a colleague, friend, or spouse until you're less tired, more composed, or less annoyed can be perfectly adaptive and healthy. Again, the problem with self-preservation strategies comes when they actively harm someone or become enshrined as our habitual response. We need to be compassionate with ourselves. Sometimes the best we can do is to simply get through a situation.

Appendix A: Some Common Questions

I've tried really hard to identify the wound that gave rise to my greed, self-justification, lust, fear, lying, gluttony, and so forth, but I can't seem to identify it. What should I do?

It's okay if we can't always identify the wound that has given rise to our self-preservation strategies. It's not detrimental to our healing if we don't remember the wound that has been at the root of our preservation strategies. After all, it's really our unhelpful reaction to the wound that is causing our anxiety, unhappiness, and stress. Let's give an example to show that identifying the wound is not as important as identifying the character defect. Imagine someone is always trying to get more money, property, or goods for themselves (greed). They aren't aware of why they crave this constant material security. People around them notice their greed and distance themselves from the individual. Now, because the individual is left feeling lonely and isolated, they adopt an insincere and ingratiating personality to try to maintain connection with others. As a result of the fake persona they've adopted, they always feel worried others won't want to be around them if they were really themselves. They also feel unhappy that they cannot express their true self. Loneliness arises from their greed, but unhappiness and anxiety arise from the insincerity. In this example, an individual adopts a self-preservation strategy to make up for the negative effects of a self-preservation strategy. Notice in this case that we don't need to really know the wound that originally gave rise to the greed as a preservation strategy. Can knowing the wound help make sense of the self-preservation strategy? Sure. If we knew the primary wound, could we invite the Lord into the wound and ask Him how He wants us to respond to the suffering in the moment? Yes. But, even if we can't figure out the wound, we still are most concerned with the character shortcomings (e.g., greed and insincerity) or distorted thinking patterns that are giving rise to the problems. So, be at peace if you can't identify all of

Appendix A: Some Common Questions

your wounds. Identifying your character defects is a victory in and of itself.

I attend weekly Mass, I pray the Rosary, I have devotions to certain saints, and I read Scripture. How can my relationship with God be bad?

Much like the question about service, our relationship with God is not so much about the number of religious behaviors we engage in as it is about the quality of our relationship. I know parents who put their kids in lots of sports, buy them the best gear, provide the nicest clothing, buy expensive toys, and travel on exotic vacations. Yet, if you asked the child, they would say that they don't have a great relationship with their parents. Merely going to Mass or praying the Rosary doesn't mean you have a secure, loving relationship with Our Lord or Our Lady. The quality of one's relationship is based on honesty, authenticity, security, trust, and total surrender in love. Many people go through religious motions, but have not examined the quality of their relationship with God. They confuse religious activity with having a heart that is in love with and surrendered to God. Our motivations for these religious activities should be rightly ordered. We should pray the Rosary because we love Our Lady or because we want to know her better and not because we merely think it's what a good Catholic should do. We should attend daily Mass because we love Our Lord and want to know His love more deeply, not because of what our friends might think of us if we don't. These steps give us a chance to be honest about our motivations and to let go of selfish motives and invite the Lord to replace them with selfless motives. So, if we realize we are only attending Mass out of fear of what our parents might think about us if we don't go, we might say to the Lord, "I see my fear and how it is motivating me, Jesus. It is blocking me from really approaching You. Please remove this motive of fear of what others might think and please instead replace it with love for You and a desire to know You better." The Lord answers prayers of such humility and poverty of spirit.

In step two you asked us to imagine God as we desire Him to be. Aren't we just making God in our image and after our likeness if we do that?

I can see how it might seem like this to some, but that is not the intention, nor is it likely to be the result of this exercise. The problem is that many of us have already made God in the image of our parents, our priest, or our spouse. We erroneously assume that God would respond to us with the attitude, tone, and in similar ways to those that these important figures responded to us. Our image of God is tainted by negative emotionally charged experiences with important figures. What we're doing is taking apart and rebuilding a healthier image of God. Where we previously overemphasized a particular characteristic (e.g., justice) of God that made approaching Him difficult, we now overemphasize a counter-characteristic (e.g., mercy, forgiveness) in order to correct our distorted image of God again. The problem is that many people are unwilling to open their hearts and trustingly surrender their lives to a God who they believe thinks, feels, and acts like the people in their lives. The second step encourages us to identify the characteristics that we desire God to possess in order for us to approach Him with an open heart. I firmly believe that once you approach God with an open, humble heart, He will lead you into a deeper understanding of Himself, correcting any misconceptions that you may hold. Many of us approach God in a superficial, shallow, fearful, or inauthentic manner, not giving ourselves to Him entirely. In this way, we cannot touch or be touched by His healing power. We have not surrendered, so we cannot be led by Him. If we can find enough safety in Him to able to surrender our ideas and attitudes to

Appendix A: Some Common Questions

His care, we will be disposed to having our ideas about who He is continually purified and shaped by Him. So the second step is about highlighting the characteristics we need to emphasize in order to open up the doors of surrender to a God we can trust.

Sometimes I pretend to be happy or peaceful or calm because I want to try to "fake it until I make it." What's wrong with that?

It depends. If "fake it until you make it" means that we should pretend that we are not feeling a certain way or deny that we have certain feelings, then I think that it is silly and can cause further emotional problems. I see Catholics sometimes pretending or faking like they aren't feeling grief, fear, or anger because they think that it means that they don't have faith, hope, or love. So, they deny that they are having these feelings and spend significant emotional energy and effort to change, suppress, or get out of these feelings. This is the unhealthy side of faking it. "Faking it until you make it" can be helpful when it refers to our behaviors, rather than our feelings. I take "fake it until we make it" to mean that we can act in healthy ways that are different or contrary to the way we feel and how we might want to act based on our feelings. I can feel angry, but choose not to hit someone and choose to speak in a respectful tone of voice. I can feel sad and lazy, but still choose to get out of bed in the morning. I can feel grief and choose not to isolate or lash out in anger. This is also where the expression "Bring the body and the mind will follow" is helpful. In many cases, though not always, if we act or behave in a healthy, mature, Christian manner, our feelings and thoughts will eventually conform to those behaviors—we act ourselves into right thinking and feeling. We shouldn't act like we're not *feeling* anger or grief; we should act in a healthy, mature manner, while acknowledging that we are feeling grief or anger. Just to reiterate, I don't think that faking as if we aren't feeling angry, sad, grief-stricken, or scared is helpful. What is helpful is not to act in unhealthy ways based on these feelings.

Can this program be done alone?

While one can certainly go through these steps alone, I genuinely believe that a program like this is best done in a group. Having a group of individuals (preferably of the same sex—men with men and women with women) with whom you can touch base and share your daily experiences can be indispensable. Doing work like this in a group provides accountability and encouragement. We are much less likely to give ourselves a pass or let ourselves slide on the spiritual principles we are trying to live by if we have a group of individuals who are trying to live the same way. Also, others can often see areas in our lives where we may need to change and heal. They can gently and lovingly challenge us, support us, and share their experiences with us. It's important that in working through these steps as a group there is no judgment, coercion, or condescension. To create the best environment for change, a person must feel supported and cared for—the group's job is to provide some of the conditions that facilitate someone starting or continuing the healing process. Ultimately, however, the group needs to step aside and let the Lord do the real work. In this way, there should be no clear leader or guide in any groups that form around these steps. Everyone is journeying together on the path to greater healing, freedom, and conversion. It is the Lord who leads.

You've mentioned that I am supposed to orient my whole life around loving and serving God and others, but how do I know what is my will and what is God's will?

Good question. If we've taken these steps seriously, we are now in the business of turning our will over to God—of

Appendix A: Some Common Questions

trying to align our will with His in all things at all times "What would you have me do right now, Lord? I am totally Yours!" Sometimes when we ask this question, we receive a strong inspiration or intuition as to what the Lord's will is for us in a particular moment. Not always, but sometimes. As we grow in the spiritual life, these inspirations often become more frequent. They do not feel earth-shattering, however. No white lights or voices. Just a peaceful sense of what should be done. That is not to say that the Lord doesn't sometimes indicate His will for us in stronger, more obvious ways (e.g., voices, visions, etc.). But, in most cases, we do not receive such explicit clarity. The question arises, however: What we should do when we don't receive even an inspiration of what God's will is for us? In such cases, it is helpful to ask whether the action we are considering brings more of God and His characteristics into a situation or not. Does our considered course of action increase the love, mercy, peace, purity, and truth in a given situation or relationship? We should not be looking to cause problems, division, or resentment among others.

Now, I'm not saying we must have peace at all costs. I can imagine some people thinking that I am not advocating for orthodox Catholicism—that I am suggesting a feel-good, watered-down version of the faith. I am not! I can, however, hear people saying, "People need to hear the truth, regardless of how they feel about it. That's what's loving." There are times when the truth must be boldly proclaimed. Yet, there is also room to use prudence to determine when, where, how, and with whom certain truths need to be shared. I'm generally convinced that we shouldn't use the truth to bludgeon people. When deliberating how we might act or what we might say or should do, many of us act out of our own fears and insecurities and thereby bring less God (and more of ourselves) into the situation. I know many faithful Catholics who are quick to correct any moral or theological error in anyone with whom they come in contact. They haven't converted a single person or brought them back into the fold, but they feel a certain satisfaction that they are telling the truth. In reality, I often find that many of these folks are not motivated by a genuine and selfless love for others, but are driven by insecurity to defend and uphold their position or to rush to the moral high ground. Sometimes, they are motivated by a desire to ease their own anxiety about failing to admonish the sinner. We must be brutally honest with ourselves about whether our motivation is a loving desire to evangelize or whether it is a self-centered desire. We will be more effective evangelists if we try to act as God would have us act, bringing love, patience, mercy, purity, and truth into a situation. Generally, using mercy and love as the principle to discern what God would have you do is a good rule: "What action will allow me to bring the most love and mercy to this situation?" Again, this does not mean that we shy away from hard or difficult conversations or action when that is indicated, but it does mean that we don't need to bring unnecessary strife, conflict, or resentment into a situation. We seek to understand others before wanting to be understood. Sometimes it's not about me *making* God's will present, but about me stepping back and letting God's will unfold.

APPENDIX B: PRAYERS

Surrender Novena

Day 1

Why do you confuse yourselves by worrying? Leave the care of your affairs to Me and everything will be peaceful. I say to you in truth that every act of true, blind, complete surrender to Me produces the effect that you desire and resolves all difficult situations.

O Jesus, I surrender myself to You, take care of everything!
(ten times)

Day 2

Surrender to Me does not mean to fret, to be upset, or to lose hope, nor does it mean offering to Me a worried prayer asking Me to follow you and change your worry into prayer. It is against this surrender, deeply against it, to worry, to be nervous, and to desire to think about the consequences of anything.

It is like the confusion that children feel when they ask their mother to see to their needs, and then try to take care of those needs for themselves so that their childlike efforts get in their mother's way. Surrender means to placidly close the eyes of the soul, to turn away from thoughts of tribulation, and to put yourself in My care, so that only I act, saying, "You take care of it."

O Jesus, I surrender myself to You, take care of everything! (ten times)

Day 3

How many things I do when the soul, in so much spiritual and material need, turns to Me, looks at Me, and says to Me, "You take care of it," then closes its eyes and rests. In pain you pray for Me to act, but that I act in the way you want. You do not turn to Me, instead, you want Me to adapt to your ideas. You are not sick people who ask the doctor to cure you, but rather sick people who tell the doctor how to. So do not act this way, but pray as I taught you in the Our Father: "Hallowed be Thy Name," that is, be glorified in my need. "Thy kingdom come," that is, let all that is in us and in the world be in accord with Your kingdom. "Thy will be done on earth as it is in heaven," that is, in our need, decide as You see fit for our temporal and eternal life. If you say to me truly: "Thy will be done," which is the same as saying: "You take care of it," I will intervene with all My omnipotence, and I will resolve the most difficult situations.

O Jesus, I surrender myself to You, take care of everything! (ten times)

Day 4

You see evil growing instead of weakening? Do not worry. Close your eyes and say to Me with faith: "Thy will be done, You take care of it." I say to you that I will take care of it, and that I will intervene as does a doctor and I will accomplish miracles when they are needed. Do you see that the sick person is getting worse? Do not be upset, but close your eyes and say, "You take care of it." I say to you that I will take care of it, and that there is no medicine more powerful than My loving intervention. By My love, I promise this to you.

Appendix B: Prayers

O Jesus, I surrender myself to You, take care of everything!
(ten times)

Day 5

And when I must lead you on a path different from the one you see, I will prepare you; I will carry you in my arms; I will let you find yourself, like children who have fallen asleep in their mother's arms, on the other bank of the river. What troubles you and hurts you immensely are your reason, your thoughts and worry, and your desire at all costs to deal with what afflicts you.

O Jesus, I surrender myself to You, take care of everything!
(ten times)

Day 6

You are sleepless; you want to judge everything, direct everything, and see to everything and you surrender to human strength, or worse—to men themselves, trusting in their intervention—this is what hinders My words and My views. Oh, how much I wish from you this surrender, to help you; and how I suffer when I see you so agitated! Satan tries to do exactly this: to agitate you and to remove you from My protection and to throw you into the jaws of human initiative. So, trust only in Me, rest in Me, surrender to Me in everything.

O Jesus, I surrender myself to You, take care of everything!
(ten times)

Day 7

I perform miracles in proportion to your full surrender to Me and to your not thinking of yourselves. I sow treasure troves of graces when you are in the deepest poverty. No person of reason, no thinker, has ever performed miracles, not even among the saints. He does divine works whosoever surrenders to God. So don't think about it anymore, because your mind is acute and for you it is very hard to see evil and to trust in Me and to not think of yourself. Do this for all your needs, do this, all of you, and you will see great continual silent miracles. I will take care of things, I promise this to you.

O Jesus, I surrender myself to You, take care of everything! (ten times)

Day 8

Close your eyes and let yourself be carried away on the flowing current of My grace; close your eyes and do not think of the present, turning your thoughts away from the future just as you would from temptation. Repose in Me, believing in My goodness, and I promise you by My love that if you say, "You take care of it," I will take care of it all; I will console you, liberate you, and guide you.

O Jesus, I surrender myself to You, take care of everything! (ten times)

Day 9

Pray always in readiness to surrender, and you will receive from it great peace and great rewards, even when I confer on you the grace of immolation, of repentance, and of love. Then what does suffering matter? It seems impossible to you? Close your eyes and say with all your soul, "Jesus, You take care of it." Do not be afraid, I will take care of things and you will bless My name by humbling yourself. A thousand prayers cannot equal one single act of surrender, remember this well. There is no novena more effective than this.

Appendix B: Prayers

O Jesus, I surrender myself to You, take care of everything!
(ten times)

Mother, I am yours now and forever.
Through you and with you
I always want to belong
completely to Jesus.

Litany of Trust

> From the belief that I have to earn Your love
> **Deliver me, Jesus.**
>
> From the fear that I am unlovable
> **Deliver me, Jesus.**
>
> From the false security that I have what it takes
> **Deliver me, Jesus.**
>
> From the fear that trusting You will leave me more destitute
> **Deliver me, Jesus.**
>
> From all suspicion of Your words and promises
> **Deliver me, Jesus.**
>
> From the rebellion against childlike dependency on You
> **Deliver me, Jesus.**
>
> From refusals and reluctances in accepting Your will
> **Deliver me, Jesus.**

Appendix B: Prayers

From anxiety about the future
Deliver me, Jesus.

From resentment or excessive preoccupation
with the past
Deliver me, Jesus.

From restless self-seeking in the present moment
Deliver me, Jesus.

From disbelief in Your love and presence
Deliver me, Jesus.

From the fear of being asked to give more than I have
Deliver me, Jesus.

From the belief that my life has no meaning or worth
Deliver me, Jesus.

From the fear of what love demands
Deliver me, Jesus.

From discouragement
Deliver me, Jesus.

That You are continually holding me, sustaining
me, loving me
Jesus, I trust in You.

That Your love goes deeper than my sins and failings
and transforms me
Jesus, I trust in You.

Appendix B: Prayers

That not knowing what tomorrow brings is an invitation to lean on You
Jesus, I trust in You.

That You are with me in my suffering
Jesus, I trust in You.

That my suffering, united to Your own, will bear fruit in this life and the next
Jesus, I trust in You.

That You will not leave me orphan, that You are present in Your Church
Jesus, I trust in You.

That Your plan is better than anything else
Jesus, I trust in You.

That You always hear me and in Your goodness always respond to me
Jesus, I trust in You.

That You give me the grace to accept forgiveness and to forgive others
Jesus, I trust in You.

That You give me all the strength I need for what is asked
Jesus, I trust in You.

That my life is a gift
Jesus, I trust in You.

Appendix B: Prayers

That you will teach me to trust You.
Jesus, I trust in You.

That You are my Lord and my God.
Jesus, I trust in You.

That I am Your beloved one.
Jesus, I trust in You.

In the name of the Father, and of the Son, and of the Holy Spirit.

Amen.[1]

---

[1] Written by the Sisters of Life. See www.SistersOfLife.org for more information.

APPENDIX C: WORKSHEET TEMPLATE

Sample Wound/My Part List

People/Organization/Institution	Harm Done	The Thwarted Good (6 S's)	My Part (Self-preservation, dishonesty, fear)
1.			
2.			
3.			
4.			
5.			
6.			
7.			

APPENDIX D: TEN COMMON THOUGHT ERRORS

Thought errors (or cognitive distortions) are patterns of inaccuracy or error in our thinking that can lead to unrealistic and unreasonable beliefs, inaccurate feelings, and unhelpful or unhealthy behaviors. They are specific ways in which our beliefs fail to take into account all the evidence available or fail to fit with the evidence we have. Thought errors affect us all, and we tend to have a few that we consistently struggle with or fall into.

1. **All-or-Nothing Thinking** The tendency to see things in extremes. Things are black and white without recognizing shades of grey. For example, you view someone as either all good or all bad; or, a situation is a total success or an absolute failure.

2. **Overgeneralization** This occurs when you take one (or a very small number) of examples or instances and generalize to apply it to all instances. For example, you've had a bad experience with *one* priest, so you assume priests in general are untrustworthy.

3. **Mental Filter** This is the tendency to only see negative information or events. You filter out positive information and experiences. For example, multiple administrators over the years have told you what a great teacher you are, but you focus on the one who gave you critical or harsh feedback without acknowledging the positive feedback on your evaluation.

Appendix D: Ten Common Thought Errors

4. **Disqualifying the Positive** Similar to the mental filter, this error occurs when you recognize positive information or experiences but reject them. For example, you have thoughts like, "They don't really like me, they're just saying that so they don't hurt my feelings."

5. **Mind Reading** This is the tendency to assume that you know what someone is thinking when in fact we have no clue unless they tell us. For example, you tell yourself, "I know that my teacher thinks my work is sloppy," even though the teacher has not said so.

6. **Fortune Telling** This occurs when we believe that we know what's going to happen based on little-to-no evidence. For example, you might say, "I'm not going to get that promotion. I just know it," even though you can't give concrete reasons for this opinion.

7. **Emotional Reasoning** This occurs when we assume that our emotions are facts. We believe that emotions signal the truth about a situation. For example, when we feel sad, we assume the situation must be a sad situation; when we are angry at a person or event our anger must be true and justified. The truth is, we should feel our feelings, but feelings aren't facts. Sometimes we have a feeling toward a person, situation, or experience that isn't consistent with the feelings we are experiencing.

8. **Catastrophizing** This is the tendency to blow things out of proportion or to make a mountain out of a molehill. It occurs when we exaggerate the significance, likelihood, or meaning of something. For example, we might think, "I made a mistake at work, so my boss is going to fire me and I'm going to end up living alone and poor my whole life." The oppositive is *minimizing*.

Appendix D: Ten Common Thought Errors

9. **"Should" Statements** This occurs when we impose beliefs on ourselves or others regarding what we "should do" or how we "should be." "Should" statements sound like this: "Men shouldn't show emotion" or "Holy people shouldn't feel angry at others."

10. **Personalization** This is the tendency to assume that everything revolves around you—that you are the cause or focus of a situation or event. It often occurs when we blame ourselves or feel criticized without recognizing that perhaps we had nothing to do with the situation (e.g., your friend is quiet and you assume it's because you've done something wrong, rather than assuming that they could be tired, sad, or preoccupied by some other thoughts).